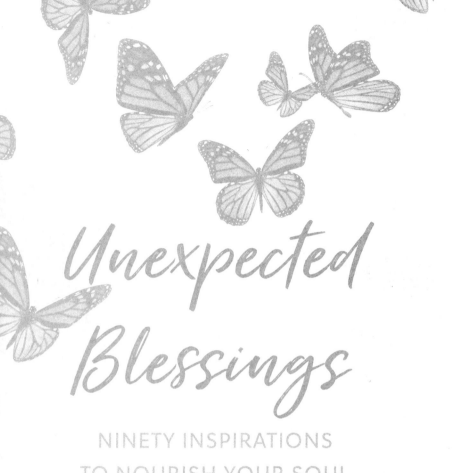

Unexpected Blessings

NINETY INSPIRATIONS TO NOURISH YOUR SOUL AND OPEN YOUR HEART

ROMA DOWNEY

HOWARD BOOKS

ATRIA

New York • London • Toronto • Sydney • New Delhi

HOWARD
BOOKS

ATRIA

An Imprint of Simon & Schuster, Inc.
1230 Avenue of the Americas
New York, NY 10020

All Scripture references, unless otherwise indicated, are taken from the Holy Bible, New International Version®, NIV® Copyright ©1973, 1978, 1984, 2011 by Biblica, Inc.® Used by permission. All rights reserved worldwide.

First Howard Books/Atria Books hardcover edition April 2022

HOWARD BOOKS/**ATRIA** B O O K S and colophon are trademarks of Simon & Schuster, Inc.

For information about special discounts for bulk purchases, please contact Simon & Schuster Special Sales at 1-866-506-1949 or business@simonandschuster.com.

The Simon & Schuster Speakers Bureau can bring authors to your live event. For more information or to book an event, contact the Simon & Schuster Speakers Bureau at 1-866-248-3049 or visit our website at www.simonspeakers.com.

Interior design by Dana Sloan

Manufactured in the United States of America

1 3 5 7 9 10 8 6 4 2

Library of Congress Cataloging-in-Publication Data has been applied for.

ISBN 978-1-9821-9922-7
ISBN 978-1-9821-9923-4 (ebook)

I'd like to dedicate this book to my beloved family:
My darling husband, Mark, my gorgeous daughter, Reilly,
and my two lovely stepsons, James and Cameron.
My blended family is an unexpected blessing
for which I am truly grateful.

Thank you for picking up a copy of my devotional, *Unexpected Blessings*. I pray that these inspirations will nourish your soul and open your heart. With each entry you read, I pray that you will hear God's loving voice.

I had such thoughtful and kind feedback from many of you about my bestselling book *Box of Butterflies*. I was inspired to take a deeper dive into the themes of that book—strength, kindness, courage, love, stillness, gratitude, and home. I created this devotional using some of the stories from my life that I shared in *Box of Butterflies*. But I also felt a nudge in my heart to share new stories as well, along with lessons I learned from them.

At the beginning of each devotional, you'll read either a small excerpt from *Box of Butterflies* or a quote I find inspirational or both. I'll share a Scripture to reflect on, and we'll explore how the two fit together to teach us God's truth, strengthening us for the day ahead. Finally, I'll lead us in a prayer to still our minds in the loving presence of God.

We all live such busy lives, and in our busyness, we can forget to take a moment for ourselves, for each other, for God. We forget to notice the sometimes-surprising blessings He sends. Yet a kind word, a sweet smile, and a tender touch are all simple and loving ways that can remind us to move through our day with grace. Remember, it only takes a moment to be kind. By committing to a daily devotional, you are showing kindness to yourself. You are taking time to be still and know God.

Unexpected Blessings is my gift to you, a gentle reminder to start each day in the presence of our loving God. I do hope the time you spend reading this book lifts your spirit and touches your heart, reminding you that you are special and loved.

I believe God wants to walk with us on a path of greater trust, greater peace, greater hope. I'm picturing this devotional as a journey you and I will take together, listening to God's voice of love. If that sounds good to you, let's close with a prayer, looking forward to all that He has in store for us.

Thank You, God, for speaking to us.
Thank You for making this beautiful world for us to enjoy.
Please help us to hear Your voice, Lord.
Teach us to be quiet and listen to Your message of love.
We want to know and love You more.
Reveal to us Your unexpected blessings and
strengthen us through every page of this book, we pray.
In Jesus' name, amen.

Take care, dear reader.
With love,

Roma

Strength

The Strength to Soar

I know that this life can be filled with sorrow.
We all experience loss and heartbreak.
But oh, if we can just remember that in the struggle our
wings become stronger.
We can get through even the hardest times, and one day
we will fly.

BOX OF BUTTERFLIES

Therefore we do not lose heart. Though outwardly we
are wasting away, yet inwardly we are being renewed
day by day . . . So we fix our eyes not on what is seen,
but on what is unseen, since what is seen is temporary,
but what is unseen is eternal.

2 CORINTHIANS 4:16, 18

I've been a person of faith my whole life. In our house it was always the right time for a prayer. Gratitude for God's blessings was part of the everyday fabric of our lives. I lost my mother suddenly when I was only ten, and our faith became even more essential as my family leaned on each other and God to get us through that difficult and painful time.

Not long after Mother passed, my father and I visited her graveside. We brought pansies, her favorite flower. She said they reminded her of little butterflies. Just then a butterfly flew right in front of us, dancing on the wind. And my dad said, "Would you look at that! That wee butterfly could be your mother's spirit right there." I have always felt that that butterfly was a gift from God, a reminder of His loving presence.[1] It was a comfort to me.

In my grief, God reminded me I wasn't alone. You are not alone in your pain, either. As we surrender our heartache to Jesus, we can find purpose in pain.

I don't imagine many caterpillars creeping about, contemplating their purpose. When they begin to spin cocoons, they probably aren't envisioning future challenges. Breaking out of a tight sheath of woven silk is difficult, but there is purpose in the caterpillar's pain. In the struggle to release itself from a dark cocoon, the butterfly becomes strong enough to fly.

I don't know what you brought to this devotional. You may be suffering deeply and struggling with overwhelming issues. My heart breaks with you. You may be enjoying a glorious season of peace. I rejoice with you.

Wherever you are in your life, I urge you to fix your eyes, not on your circumstances but on Jesus. At some point, all of us face the dark cocoon of pain. We may long to escape. Yet we must also remember that our struggle, in the hands of God, has purpose. In this way, pain becomes an unexpected blessing. It makes us strong enough to fly.

Dear Jesus, please help me to fix my eyes on You,
not on what's around me.
Thank You that even when I feel like I'm
wasting away,
You are with me.
You bring hope and peace in the dark.
Help me to find Your purpose in every
heartache.
Please make me strong enough to fly with You,
and please help me encourage others to soar
with You, too.
Amen.

The Strength to Remember

I remember it so clearly . . . I read through a number of scripts that my agent wanted me to consider; none was terribly appealing. Then I picked up one with the working title Angel's Attic, *later to be retitled* Touched by an Angel.

BOX OF BUTTERFLIES

. . . the Holy Spirit, Whom the Father will send in My name, will teach you all things and will remind you of everything I have said to you.

JOHN 14:26

Memory allows us to revisit the most beautiful moments of our lives. I'll never forget receiving the audition packet for *Touched by an Angel*. Far more significantly, I recall the breathtaking moment I held Reilly, my daughter, for the very first time. And I'm still tempted to blush as I recall stealing glances at my husband, Mark, before I even knew his name (and while he was getting a haircut, no less). I cherish the recollection of my mother singing and laughing, the way poetry came alive as my father read it to me, night after night.

Other memories, of course, carry a tremendous amount of pain. All of us would like to forget some things.

May I also propose that you and I might have forgotten some things that God wants us to remember?

Years ago, when I read the pilot script for *Touched by an Angel*, tears came to my eyes. This was the kind of material I had been looking for. The series told the story of angels who show up at crossroads in people's lives with a message of faith and love. The angels come to earth to remind people that God loves them and hasn't forgotten them.[2]

Jesus must have known people would need help remembering what He said; that's why John 14:26 promises the Holy Spirit will *teach* us and *remind* us. I don't know about you, but I often need reminding. Just like the people my character, Monica, visited in each episode of *Touched by an Angel*, I often need to be reminded that God loves me, that He hasn't forgotten me.

I believe God wants you to remember this, too.

As we journey together, I hope to help you remember. I pray that I can remind you of truths you may have forgotten in the busyness and strain of life. I want to point you to our eternal home.

In this process, God may ask us to lay certain memories aside. He doesn't want those recollections to hurt us any longer. We can let go; we can forgive. Our memories can be shaped by God. Today we can choose to take up His peace. We can be reminded of His love. I'd like to pray for us as we choose.

Father, thank You for reminding us who we are
and Whose we are.
We are Your beloved children.
May we never forget that You are
for us and with us.
Please use the words in this book and in Your
Book to teach and remind us every day.
You are the source of all that is good,
beautiful, and true.
We love You and we receive Your strength.
In Jesus' name, amen.

The Strength of a Compassionate Heart

I realized that playing the role of Monica would require a compassionate heart. And I felt deep in my soul that I had been prepared for this role by the loss I had experienced in my own life.

BOX OF BUTTERFLIES

Jesus saw the huge crowd as He stepped from the boat, and He had compassion on them and healed their sick.

MATTHEW 14:14

Never underestimate the strength of a compassionate heart. It requires very little of a person to be self-focused, bitter, or angry. Compassion, on the other hand, asks quite a lot of us. It requires us to look outward and upward, to receive strength from God and freely give His love to others.

I grew up watching my father display a thousand small acts of compassion. His example shaped me. Playing Monica on *Touched by an Angel* for nine seasons expanded my compassionate heart even further.

In each episode, I knew that I could relate to the very people Monica was coming to visit, that I could meet those people in their places of loss and hurt because I had felt loss and hurt so intensely myself at such a young age.[3] In God's hands, the pain of losing my mother was not wasted, but transformed into a heart of compassion.

Over and again, the Bible describes Jesus as compassionate. He saw hurting people and healed them. He saw anxious people and spoke words of peace. He saw downhearted people and gave them hope.

I believe that, if we look around, we will see the same kinds of people—hurting, harried, hopeless. Like Jesus, we can respond to them with compassion, if only we will ask Him for the strength to look beyond ourselves.

This can be difficult if you have experienced deep heartache. When we lose a loved one, endure horrors like abuse or neglect, or face chronic illness, it's understandable that looking to the needs of others isn't always our first response.

That's precisely why we need Jesus to give us the strength of His compassionate heart. Only then can we give compassion to others.

The dictionary defines compassion as "a feeling of deep sympathy and sorrow for another who is stricken by misfortune, accompanied by a strong desire to alleviate the suffering."[4] What do you think might happen in our world if we prayed that God would grant us compassion—"a strong desire to alleviate suffering"? I invite you to pray with me about this right now.

Jesus, thank You for being so compassionate.
You see people and want to care for them.
Then You do!
How wonderful You are.
Thank You for caring for me so tenderly.
Please give me a beautiful heart like Yours.
Strengthen me with compassion for others,
and move in me to help the people around me,
just as You do.
Amen.

The Strength of Openness to God

My favorite part of each episode was filming the scene we called the "angel revelation." Monica was an undercover angel pretending to be a doctor or a police officer, but she was truly there to help someone at an emotional crossroads. The moment always came when the person broke down, feeling lost in the midst of their painful circumstances, before finally fully surrendering to God. They would cry out: "I cannot do this by myself. God help me."

BOX OF BUTTERFLIES

I pray that the eyes of your heart may be enlightened in order that you may know the hope to which He has called you.

EPHESIANS 1:18A

The "angel revelation" was the central, emotional heart of each episode of *Touched by an Angel*. In a person's moment of greatest need, my character, Monica, would reveal her true identity as an angel sent from Almighty God. She was a messenger, and the message was this: "There is a God, He loves you, and He has a plan for your life."

Before filming this scene, I would close my eyes, open my heart, and pray. It was an emotional moment to film, but it also filled me up—so much so that I would leave the set feeling as if God had just touched me personally. This was the moment in the show when people opened their eyes and felt the truth they had forgotten: that each of us is a special child of a loving God—a child who is loved unconditionally.[5]

What if an angel came to you, dear one? Would you open your eyes and your heart to God's message of love?

The Apostle Paul prayed that his brothers and sisters in Christ would open their eyes. Indeed, he prayed "that the eyes of [their] heart may be enlightened." This reminds me of Jesus' words in Matthew 6: "The eye is the lamp of the body; so then, if your eye is clear, your whole body will be full of light."[6]

If we want to be full of light, we need to open our eyes to God's truth. If we close our hearts to the messages of God's love, we will never know the hope to which He's called us. God wants us to develop the strength to open our eyes and hearts to Him.

In nature, through relationships, in His Word, through prayer, God is sending light and love to fill you. Open your eyes today, dear one. Let His light flood in.

Heavenly Father, thank You for revealing Yourself to me.
You open Your arms wide to receive me in love.
Thank You; forever thank You.
Please open my eyes to Your truth and
fill every part of me with Your light.
And please allow me to speak Your message of
hope and peace to others.
In Jesus' name, amen.

The Strength to Do All Things

The White family was shocked to learn during the reunion that they were given only a five percent chance of surviving.

CNN NEWS

I can do everything through Christ, Who gives me strength.

PHILIPPIANS 4:13, NLT

Everything? Really?

Are you saying that God can help someone learn—midair—to fly a plane on a rapid crash course?

Yes, He can.

He already has.

Just moments after pilot Lt. Col. Joe Cabuk settled his King Air twin-engine toward cruising altitude, the unimaginable happened. Cabuk suffered a massive heart attack, dying instantly. Passenger and pharmacist Doug White discovered the pilot slumped over his controls and immediately radioed for emergency support.

"Disengage the autopilot. We're gonna have you hand-fly the plane," the responding air traffic controller instructed White.

14

Months previously, God began to develop in Doug White the strength to bring his family safely to ground. White had received some private pilot lessons but had never flown anything like the sophisticated airplane in which his family traveled that fateful day. One report likened it to learning to drive a Volkswagen, then being asked to race an IndyCar twenty minutes later.[7]

God also instilled in White the steady demeanor and determined mind that enabled him to react to crisis in a truly remarkable way. "He was like the coolest cucumber," an air traffic controller remembered.

Doug White called his disposition "focused fear." What an incredible description! With a deadpan Louisiana twang, Doug White radioed Air Traffic Control: "You find me the longest, widest runway you can, ma'am . . . Me and the good Lord are hand-flying this."[8]

Doug told his wife and daughters, "Y'all go back there, and I want you to pray hard."

God answered their prayers, and their father safely landed the plane.

The Whites, longtime believers in Jesus, readily acknowledge that God brought them home through the power of prayer and strength of spirit. That's why—as one of the producers for the cinematic retelling of this miraculous story of strength, hope, and overcoming—I chose the film title *On a Wing and a Prayer*.

These events occurred on an Easter Sunday, and I believe that God arranged even the date of this miracle. Jesus' resurrection broke the power of death. His resurrection gives us hope that all things are possible. His strength in us means that far more than all we ask for or imagine is available to us through Jesus, even if that means midair flight lessons.

Dear one, whatever incredible odds you are facing or might ever face, you can do all things through Christ, Who gives you strength. Never forget it.

Thank You, Almighty God,
for granting us strength to do all things.
Sometimes life feels overwhelming.
We don't think we can make it through
certain things.
You promise that all things are possible
because of You.
Help us to fully believe and trust this.
We place our hope in Your strength
and we receive Your strength for our journey.
Amen.

The Strength to Be Still

When we're caught up in the busyness of our lives, we forget our true role in this life. When we're wrapped up in worrying about the future or are stressed about something we did in the past, we do not feel God's peace. But if we can simply stop and be in the now, we can remember Him.

BOX OF BUTTERFLIES

I recall all You have done, O Lord;
I remember Your wonderful deeds of long ago.

PSALM 77:11, NLT

While we were filming an "angel revelation" scene, it often felt as if time stood still. We would hold hands before we filmed and we would pray. All that mattered was surrendering to Love and Hope. In our surrender was a moment of remembering.

In remembering God, we come to a point of stillness, and it is in our stillness that God comes in. It is in the silence that we hear the whisper of His voice.[9] God's goodness is all too easy to forget in our noisy, worried world.

When we're overwhelmed or stressed, it's challenging to stay centered, isn't it?

It takes great strength to reject worries about the past or fears of the future. It takes strength to be in the moment, surrendered and still. But God is in the *now*! I don't want to miss Him, and I don't believe you want that, either.

I've discovered that remembering what God's done and thanking Him for it helps me stay grounded. Psalm 77:11 provides a great example of this. The Psalmist deliberately decides to "recall" all that the Lord has done and "remember" not only the good things that happened yesterday but wonderful deeds of "long ago."

God the Holy Spirit develops gratitude in us by reminding us of all He's done. Maybe you can be grateful today for that conversation you had with a beloved friend or family member. Perhaps gratitude wells up inside you recalling how God helped you financially or with a health issue. Whether you're going through a hard time or a happy time right this moment, you can always remember what Jesus did for you "long ago." He died to give you eternal life.

Right here, right now, take a moment to remember God. Let go of the busyness. Let go of worry. Recall God's love and peace. Let go of the past and be present with Jesus. Let gratitude fill your heart and give you strength.

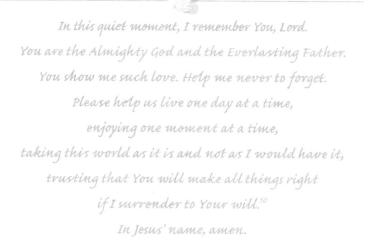

In this quiet moment, I remember You, Lord.

You are the Almighty God and the Everlasting Father.

You show me such love. Help me never to forget.

Please help us live one day at a time,

enjoying one moment at a time,

taking this world as it is and not as I would have it,

trusting that You will make all things right

if I surrender to Your will.[10]

In Jesus' name, amen.

The Strength to Press On

In three words, I can sum up everything
I've learned about life:
It goes on.

ROBERT FROST, DURING HIS EIGHTIETH BIRTHDAY CELEBRATION[11]

Forgetting what is behind and straining toward what
is ahead, I press on toward the goal to win the prize for
which God has called me heavenward in Christ Jesus.

PHILIPPIANS 3:13B–14

My mother-in-law continually impresses me. Well into her nineties, Jean lives alone, caring not only for herself but also for her beloved dog, Frank. Jean embodies two national traits of her home country, Great Britain: courage and determination. Raised during World War II, evacuated in the London Blitz amid heavy bombing by the Nazi air force, Jean developed early on the "stiff upper lip" for which Brits are famous. She also has a delicious sense of humor, and it has served her well.

I've watched Jean persevere through many trials. Her husband, Archie, faded into the painful oblivion of Alzheimer's as he neared the end of his earthly journey. She's faced loss after loss, as she's outlived so many of her loved ones. And through it all, Jean goes on.

Why? Because life goes on.

Some years ago, "resilience" became a buzzword. Businesses and schools determined people lacked resilience and scrambled to instill it into workers and children. Apparently, as a society, we had strayed from this key virtue, developed during dark times our ancestors, like Jean, experienced.

People find out what they're made of when their strength flags or fails. Like Winston Churchill, who claimed the British did not survive "because we are made of sugar candy,"[12] my mother-in-law learned that you *must* get up and brush yourself off when life hits hard; you *must* press on.

God gives us the strength to do this. And the Apostle Paul gives us the "how" in Philippians 3. We refuse to look back, fretting over the past. Instead, we "press on toward the goal to win the prize for which God has called [us] heavenward in Christ Jesus." We've been called by God, and God never calls us to something that He doesn't also empower us to do. He gives strength and resilience, courage and determination to all who will receive it.

Some days Jean doesn't want to get up. Frank helps her in this. Her sweet dog needs to be fed and walked, so Jean presses on for and with him. What helps you press on? If someone or something doesn't immediately come to mind, why not pray about it? God is calling you to a resilient, faithful life. And He will strengthen you to live it. Please allow for me to pray for us right now.

Lord, You are perfectly faithful.
Your strength never flags or fails.
We're human, Lord, and our strength often
falters,
but You have promised to empower us to the
end.
You give us new strength as we look to You.
If anyone reading needs hope or a vision of
what to press on for,
please give them that today.
We're trusting You in all things.
In Jesus' name, amen.

The Strength of Humility

It was such a privilege to bring that message of unconditional love to a nation full of viewers for so many years . . .
Before we would film, we would pray as a cast and crew.
My personal prayer was always, "Less of me, more of You."

BOX OF BUTTERFLIES

He must become greater; I must become less.

JOHN 3:30

Can you imagine someone in a boardroom, audition, or election opening with the words "Jesus must become greater; I must become less"? In our "me-first" world, living by these humble words almost seems impossible.

Dear one, humility is *not* impossible. In fact, "more of Jesus and less of me" is the pathway to greater peace.

I pray, *Less of me, more of You*, while filming or producing, parenting or grocery-shopping. No matter what I'm doing, I need the strength of Christ more than I need personal empowerment. My strength goes only so far; His power is limitless.

What about you?

Are you looking within to find purpose and power or are you looking up to God?

The Bible records John the Baptist saying, "He must become greater; I must become less." Here's the context of that verse: people who had previously come to John to learn about God now followed Jesus, and John's disciples were frustrated about that. They didn't want their leader to lose his position; they didn't want to lose their place, either.

Sometime later, Jesus' disciples are squabbling among themselves. Jesus asks, "What were you arguing about?" (Mark 9:33), "but they kept quiet because . . . they had argued about who was the greatest" (9:34). What happens next is amazing! Jesus doesn't scold them for wanting to be great. Instead, He tells them *how* to be great: Be like a child, open to the world in wonder. Spend yourself in love, serving others.

As my dear friend Pastor Rick Warren says, *"It's not about you. The purpose of your life is far greater than your own personal fulfillment, your peace of mind, or even your happiness. It's far greater than your family, your career, or even your wildest dreams and ambitions. If you want to know why you were placed on this planet, you must begin with God. You were born by His purpose and for His purpose."*[13]

Life isn't about me. It's about God. *That's* why I pray, *More of You, less of me.* Will you pray that with me right now?

You are the Almighty God,
but You came to the earth in humility.
You loved us so much that You died for us.
Lord, please help us to want
more of You and less of ourselves.
You show us the way to live and equip us to live it well.
Help us to be humble in this pride-filled world.
We need Your strength, Lord.
In Jesus' name, amen.

The Strength of a New Perspective

I have always done my best thinking by the sea. And I often take my worries to the ocean's edge and quietly pray while I walk on the sand. Something about the vast expanse of water helps to put my troubles in proper perspective. In the grand scheme of things, all the concerns I have suddenly don't seem so critical.

BOX OF BUTTERFLIES

Don't copy the behavior and customs of this world, but let God transform you into a new person by changing the way you think. Then you will learn to know God's will for you, which is good and pleasing and perfect.

ROMANS 12:2, NLT

"Change your perspective, change your life," it's oft been said. I couldn't agree more. How we view our circumstances, how we respond to what happens to us, what we choose to focus our attention on . . . these form the foundation on which we build our lives.

Standing on the shore, watching the tide roll in and out, helps adjust my perspective. I hear the greatness of God in the ocean's roar;

I know His mighty power in the crashing waves. Like the Psalmist, I can praise the Lord when I'm near the sea. "Mightier than the thunders of many waters, mightier than the waves of the sea, the Lord on high is mighty!" (Psalm 93:4, ESV).

Where can you go to get a change of perspective, my friend?

Perhaps the mighty mountains provide a sense of God's strength and solidity for you. Maybe hiking in a quiet forest, where the wind of God's Spirit blowing through a canopy of lush trees draws you nearer to Jesus, altering your view of things. You may find a change of perspective in a quilt shop, where the beautiful designs remind you of God, or while listening to a piece of uplifting music.

Wherever or whatever enables you to see things from their proper perspective . . . return to these. The strength of renewed perspective simply cannot be overstated.

When we're being honest, we also can acknowledge that certain things keep us mired in unhealthy perspectives. Though it might be difficult, we may need to pull away from certain activities, places, or even relationships that keep us from seeing life from God's perspective.

God has something to say about this in Romans 12:2. He commands us not to be formed by the world, but to let His perspective change us, to let Him transform us into new people by changing the way we think. An amazing gift comes with our adjusted perspective: knowledge of God's will—His good, pleasing, and perfect will. Trading my bad perspective for His perfect one? That's sounds like a good deal to me. What about you?

Heavenly Father, thank You for
renewing our minds.
Thank You for helping us to see things
from Your perspective.
You are so kind to us.
You want the best for us.
Thank You!
Please help us to keep choosing Your
perspective, every day.
In Jesus' name, amen.

The Strength of Simplicity

*On day trips or family outings, we would visit the
little seaside town of Moville, and after a full day of
playing on the beach or walking along the shore toward
Greencastle, we'd end up having our evening meal at a
nice family-run hotel.*

BOX OF BUTTERFLIES

*. . . the Lord has told you what is good,
and this is what He requires of you:
to do what is right, to love mercy,
and to walk humbly with your God.*

MICAH 6:8, NLT

When I was a child, it felt so swanky to eat out and have
a waiter serve us. I now have the good fortune to eat
out regularly, but back then this was a total luxury.
My brother, Lawrence, and I would order steak and chips, and our
ketchup was served in these little silver bowls. And as a special treat,
we were allowed to order a bottle of Coca-Cola or Fanta Orange.
We'd go home tired from all the sea air and meat and potatoes.[14]

My brother and I loved the simple pleasures of a cold soda and
tiny silver serving bowls, brimful with ketchup to dip our fries (which
we call "chips" in Ireland). We took very little for granted back then.
We enjoyed everything that was given to us.

There's a beautiful strength to simplicity, isn't there? A strength we so often miss in our chaotically busy, more-is-better, the-person-who-dies-with-the-most-toys-wins society. When we peel away all the trappings of modern life, however, I believe we're wired by God for what is simple and good—the butterfly, the ocean, even ketchup in miniature silver bowls.

Perhaps God has wired us this way because He asks us to follow simple principles as we walk the road of life. Of course, we can delve into rich theological discussions; I'm not saying God isn't divinely deep. The way He invites us to live, however, can be summed up in simple terms.

Reread the verse from Micah 6. What does the prophet say that the Lord requires of us? He tells us expressly—do what is right; love mercy; walk humbly.

Can you imagine how different our world would be if people operated on these simple principles? Can you imagine the strength that living in this simplicity might give you?

Sometimes we overcomplicate the life of faith. Humans construct all kinds of systems and rituals, but God simply wants us to walk with Him—in humility, kindness, righteousness, and truth. It's so freeing to live in His simplicity. Will you join me in praying that we cultivate the strength of simplicity today?

Heavenly Father, thank You for giving us so many simple joys.
Please help me to keep my eyes open for
all the simple pleasures of living.
Thank You for not making Your will and ways overly complicated.
I want to walk humbly, to love mercy, and to do what is right.
Please help me to do this in Your name.
Amen.

The Strength to Reach Out

I heard my aunt say quietly to the driver,
"My best friend, Maureen O'Reilly, just died.
Those are her w'anes back there."
It was the first time I had heard those words spoken out loud.

BOX OF BUTTERFLIES

For I am the Lord your God
Who takes hold of your right hand
and says to you, "Do not fear;
I will help you."

ISAIAH 41:13

I remember riding home in a taxi that horrible day. It was stormy and bleak. I stared out the rain-flecked window, feeling more alone than I ever dreamed possible. My brother, Lawrence, and I sat in the backseat of the cab, and my mom's best friend, whom we called Auntie Maureen, sat in the front seat with the driver. She told him the truth of what happened that day: my mother had just died. The shock of hearing those words out loud pierced me.

Without looking at one another, my brother and I reached across the backseat of the taxi and clasped each other's hands, knowing our lives had been changed forever.

This memory seared itself in my mind and heart. It became a visceral picture of what virtually every suffering person instinctively does. We reach out for a hand to hold. Over the course of my life, I've grieved the loss of many loved ones who've gone home ahead of me. I've experienced pain in so many ways common to mankind, yet I can genuinely say that, if we have an open heart, there is always a hand to hold.

Isaiah 41:13 affirms this astounding promise: God Himself takes hold of our hand. He calms our anxious hearts. He speaks peace over our turbulent lives: *Do not fear; I will help you.*

How do you respond to this promise today? Do you have confidence that you can reach out to God, that—indeed—He is already and always reaching out to you?

You may or may not have grown up believing there was a hand to hold. You may have lived with painful loneliness. Whatever you have previously experienced, Jesus is reaching out to you *this very moment*, urging you to let Him hold your hand and quiet your fears. He also offers you the chance—as part of the human family—to learn how to reach out to others.

Some days you are the one who needs a hand to hold. Some days your hand will be the one someone else desperately needs. Will you take a moment and ask God which role He might have for you today?

Precious Father, thank You for reaching out to us.
Thank You for giving us a hand to hold . . . always.
Please help me cultivate the strength to reach out
when I'm hurting
and to be there for others when things are going well for me.
Is there someone You want me to reach out to today, Lord?
I trust You to give me every ounce of strength I need.
In Jesus' name, amen.

The Strength to Shine

There she was, wearing bright and colorful
clothing that was nothing compared to the luminous
smile she wore on her face.
She radiated love and warmth and joy.

BOX OF BUTTERFLIES

Those who are wise will shine like the brightness of the
heavens, and those who lead many to righteousness, like
the stars for ever and ever.

DANIEL 12:3

We filmed the pilot episode of *Touched by an Angel* in Wilmington, North Carolina. It was there that I first met Miss Della Reese. I was eager to meet her, having heard so much about her, and I was so looking forward to working closely with her. Of course we would be angels on-screen together, but in my heart I was hoping we would be more than that; I was hoping that we would be friends.

My first encounter with Della was in the makeup trailer, where her radiance filled the trailer and spilled over me. I was awed and slightly intimidated at first, so I approached her quietly, politely reaching out my hand and saying, "I just wanted to introduce myself."

"Oh, baby, I don't shake hands, I hug." Della smiled. And she

wrapped me in the biggest, most loving embrace I had ever experienced. I immediately felt comfortable and at ease.

In some ways, Della and I were an unlikely duo—a brassy and bold Black singer from downtown Detroit and a small, soft-spoken white woman from Ireland—yet our strong faith formed a deeper bond than any difference could separate us. We loved and strengthened one another for decades, not merely on air, but in everyday life as well.

Della embodied the verse from Daniel 12 that I included earlier. In this particular chapter of Scripture, Daniel prophesies the end of all time, when the righteous will receive the promise of eternal life. He foretells the wise shining "like the brightness of the heavens." Della didn't wait until the end of time to radiate; she shone with heavenly light every day, and the strength of her faith influenced many to know and love God.

Of course, I knew Della wasn't perfect. She was human just like the rest of us. But the strength, warmth, wisdom, and love I experienced in her friendship and the joy I found in our collaborative work impacted me deeply. Being around Della—with all her feisty and formidable strength, not to mention her fierce loyalty and protectiveness—made me a better woman, a better friend, a better follower of Christ.

I pray that I might be to others what Della was to me. I'm different from Della. I have different gifts, different strengths, but I pray that what God's given me, a strength that is uniquely "me," will help others see the Light of the World more clearly. What about you? What message does your life currently send? Let's pray about this now.

Jesus, You are the Light of the World.
You shine through all Your beloved children.
Thank You for making each one of us unique.
Thank You for giving each of us
a light to carry
into a world that's often dark.
Please strengthen us, that we might
help others to know You, love You,
and walk with You.
Amen.

The Strength to Be Present

"I won't say a word. I'll just be here with you the whole way, holding your hand."

BOX OF BUTTERFLIES

The Lord replied, "My Presence will go with you, and I will give you rest."

EXODUS 33:14

I threw open the door to Della's trailer. Nothing could have prepared me to see my co-star, the woman who had become my second mother, bereft with grief. She repeated only one phrase: "She's gone; she's gone." The inimitable Della Reese, the off-the-charts-talented Della Reese, the sassy and strong Della Reese, collapsed into my arms, sobbing.

Della's only daughter had just passed into eternity.

I knew instantly that Della needed to get home to her husband. I helped her change out of her costume and into an airport transfer. As we sank into the backseat, Della took my hand in hers. "I don't want to talk," she said quietly, turning to gaze out the window.[15]

We held hands in silence. I prayed in silence.

At the airport, I made sure she had space to grieve, undisturbed by adoring fans. I helped her onto the plane with as few words as possible. As she slept briefly on the flight, I quietly pleaded with our Heavenly Father to give her rest and peace.

Through this tragedy, I experienced the strength of silence, the strength of presence.

In those moments, Della didn't need me to have the perfect words, nor even the perfect prayer or Bible verse. She needed the strength of my hand pressed in hers, the strength of my quiet presence. The strength of a love that can be silent as tears fall.

Presence is powerful.

Exodus 33:14 helps us understand why. This verse tells us that God's presence ushers us into restful peace. So, when we are present with others, as our Heavenly Father is ever present with us, we help them enter His rest and peace.

Do you know someone suffering today?

Would you take a quiet moment to ask God how He might want you to be present for that person?

Sometimes we shrink back when people are hurting; we're afraid we'll say or do something wrong. That's understandable. We're human, after all, and we don't always have the right words or know the best next step.

If you're a believer in Jesus, however, you can bring His presence to someone, even if you don't speak a word. Don't worry about solving things. Simply be present, dear one, and God can use you to help someone move from pain to peace.

Father, Your Word promises that
You are an ever-present help in time of trouble.
Thank You for being close and for loving me
so much, especially when I'm hurting.
There are so many heartbroken people
in our world, Lord.
Your presence is near, but many can't feel it.
Sometimes I can't feel You.
Please help me to trust that You are close
and bring Your loving and peaceful
presence to others.
In Jesus' name, amen.

Kindness

Kindness Is Always Possible

A simple act of kindness on my part might be the very thing a person needs, the very thing to remind them that they are not alone.

BOX OF BUTTERFLIES

I tell you, love your enemies. Help and give without expecting a return. You'll never—I promise—regret it. Live out this God-created identity the way our Father lives toward us, generously and graciously, even when we're at our worst. Our Father is kind; you be kind.

LUKE 6:35, MSG

Kindness is important to me . . . extremely important.

The email signature I chose constantly reminds me, as a person of faith, of my high call to no-matter-what kindness. The beautiful and challenging words "Be kind whenever possible. It is always possible" appear at the end of each email I write.

I believe this. I believe it's always possible to be kind.

Not that it's always *easy*. Possible doesn't mean *simple*. It simply means possible.

What about you, dear one? Do you believe it's possible to be kind no matter what the circumstances, no matter who the person, no matter how unkindly you've been treated?

Jesus showed us that kindness is always possible.

When Mark and I brought the Bible to television, some of the most amazing and heart-wrenching scenes to film involved Jesus responding—without retaliating—to those torturing and falsely accusing Him. Christ could have called down legions of angels to fight on His behalf. Vengeance could have been His. Instead, He cried out from the Cross:

"Father, forgive them, for they do not know what they are doing" (Luke 23:34).

Can you imagine showing kindness to your enemies on this scale? For many of us, it's difficult to conceive of, yet our world is full of stories of those who forgive and extend kindness, even in appalling situations. A mother speaks words of kindness to her child's attacker. Victims choose love rather than hate. Kindness is possible *even in the most trying of circumstances.*

Of course, kindness doesn't mean zero consequences. Kindness doesn't erase what happened or let people off the hook. Instead, kindness sets you and me free from the bitterness threatening to corrode our hearts when we've been wronged.

Luke 6:35 makes clear that kindness is always possible because our Heavenly Father is kind. He gives without expectation of return. He lives generously and graciously toward us even when we're at our worst. Isn't that wonderful? When you choose kindness, "You'll never—I promise—regret it."

Kindness is part of your God-created identity. Will you live this out?

Help us, Lord.

Help us to become vessels of

Your love, Your peace, Your Spirit . . .

Not just to those who are easy to love,

Not just to those we think belong to us,

but to all Your children.

May we be part of a kindness revolution,

in Your name,

and smile by smile, hug by hug,

change the world.

In Jesus' name, amen.[16]

Kindness in Every Moment

*Not all of us can do great things, but we can do
small things with great love.*

MOTHER TERESA

Love is patient. Love is kind . . .

1 CORINTHIANS 13:4A

They looked like children to me, the paramedics wheeling my beloved Della Reese into the ambulance. I tried to engage them in a bit of conversation about the precious woman they had been entrusted to transport back home—likely for the last time—but both young men seemed detached. Professional, but distant.

My heart ached for Della, who would be returning home without her husband, Franklin. He, too, was ailing, and needed to remain in the hospital. I promised to get Della home safely and rode in the back of the ambulance, heavy with the knowledge that I would soon lose my dear friend.

When we arrived at the Reese-Lett house and the paramedics lowered Della's gurney, I felt agitated by their cold disengagement. *Don't you know how amazing this woman is?* my heart silently cried. We walked in silence, the unusual clouds covering Los Angeles that day a gray shroud reflecting my soul's sadness.

In an instant, a burst of sunshine shone through the clouds.

"Please. Please, stop," I begged the paramedics.

Della always loved the sun; she loved to feel its warmth, and I knew this might be the final time she felt its rays on her beautiful face.

42

Thankfully, the young men paused. Della—who had been in and out of consciousness—clearly responded, relishing the light and heat. The sun illuminated this precious woman, a woman who had shown me such extraordinary love, who modeled a faith in Jesus that inspired me every day I knew her.

Instantly the paramedics were present . . . fully present. The emotion might have been awe. The atmosphere was certainly holy.

"Thank you, baby," Della breathed.

That holy moment, shared with two paramedics, will be seared into my mind forever.

It was a small thing—stopping to allow my friend to feel the sun on her face—but love converted that small thing into a transformative moment. Love is patient and kind, First Corinthians tells us. Let's not hurry through life so quickly that we miss the chance to show kindness in a million small ways, all of which become great in Jesus' hands.

We can also be on the lookout for the small and great ways God reveals His loving-kindness: in a burst of sunshine . . . in a thank-you offered from a cherished friend . . . or in moments so sacred they can hardly be expressed in words. When God invites us into these moments, our best—perhaps our only right—response is to offer Him grateful worship and pass His love onto others. Let's commit to that in prayer.

Lord, there is none like You.

Thank You for revealing Your love in small and great things.

I don't want to miss anything, Father.

I love You dearly and deeply.

Please help me to patiently and kindly love others.

I trust You to help me do that.

In Jesus' name, amen.

Kindness That Goes Beyond

When I was a boy and I would see scary things in the news, my mother would say to me, "Look for the helpers. You will always find people who are helping."

FRED ROGERS[17]

This is what the Lord of Heaven's Armies says: Judge fairly, and show mercy and kindness to one another. Do not oppress widows, orphans, foreigners, and the poor. And do not scheme against each other.

ZECHARIAH 7:9–10, NLT

Forty-three years.

That's how long Fred Rogers's classic TV show for children, *Mister Rogers' Neighborhood*, ran on PBS. Rogers was a puppeteer and ordained minister who also held a degree in music composition. He wrote two hundred songs for the show, including the iconic theme, "Won't You Be My Neighbor?" Rogers won numerous awards and accolades for his dedication to children, including the Presidential Medal of Freedom.

For over four decades, Fred Rogers committed himself to helping young people—and their parents—make sense of complex issues. "The world is not always a kind place," Rogers observed. "That's something all children learn for themselves, whether we want them to or not, but it's something they really need our help to understand."

When was the first time you remember experiencing that "the world is not always a kind place"? It's a sad and scary thing to acknowledge, isn't it?

Just as his mom urged him to do, Rogers encouraged children to look for the helpers when confronted with frightening news. It helps for grown-ups to identify for children the people who are doing the work of kindness and restoration. As adults, we are also invited by God to take a step beyond looking for the helpers.

God wants you to *be* a helper, too.

Zechariah 7:9–10 instructs us to judge fairly, showing mercy and kindness. God also warns us not to mistreat (oppress) the poor, the needy, the powerless. We act like the Lord of Heaven when we choose kindness, when we help rather than hurt others. Psalm 46:1 tells us that God Himself is an "ever present help in trouble." He is always there to help, and He enables us to be a help for others facing heartache and hopelessness.

The modern world is full of plenty of frightening news. There *will* be a day when fear, struggle, and pain will be no longer. Until that day, God calls us to be part of the solution, part of his army of helpers. Are you currently accepting His invitation to help? In the battle against trouble in this world, kindness is your sword.

Lord, may I be reminded of Your presence in my life.
May I have the eyes to see the needs of Your people.
May I have a heart to feel their hurts
and the willingness to see how I may help.
May I seek to be a bringer of light.
May kindness be my mantle and my sword as
I walk through this world.
In Jesus' name, amen.[18]

Kindness Is God's Heart for Humanity

I was born in Derry City, Northern Ireland, a beautiful border town in the North West of Ireland. Yet throughout my childhood, my town was filled with tension and violence that began when I was about eight years old. I grew up in the midst of a war that became known in Ireland as "the Troubles."

BOX OF BUTTERFLIES

For He Himself is our peace, Who has made the two groups one and has destroyed the barrier, the dividing wall of hostility.

EPHESIANS 2:14

The Troubles was a war between neighboring people wanting different things and being unable to find common ground. One group desired independence from the United Kingdom, hoping to become part of the Republic of Ireland (Republicans); while the other wanted to remain a part of the United Kingdom (Loyalists). Both sides harbored animosity, distrust, and prejudice toward each other.[19]

The situation in Northern Ireland has greatly improved, but, sadly, trouble plagues many places in the world today, even in our own country. Animosity, distrust, prejudice toward each other . . . we see it everywhere.

It breaks my heart to see this anger and prejudice toward others happening all over the world today. I imagine it breaks God's heart infinitely more.

On our own, human beings are not the kindest of creatures. But *with Jesus,* all of that can change. Read again the verse that opens today's devotional. Christ is not only able to destroy the barriers between us and the dividing walls of hostility; it's His eternal plan to do so. Unity is His purpose because unity brings His peace.

Kindness is the very heart of God toward humanity. Ephesians 2:7 describes the "incredible wealth of His grace and kindness toward us" (NLT). If this is Who God is and we are His children, shouldn't we start showing more kindness and less animosity toward our neighbors, more patience and less prejudice?

We cannot save the entire world, but, one act of kindness at a time, we can make a difference. Let's not be paralyzed by the huge needs or overwhelmed by all the pain—and end up doing nothing. We must do something, and if we each do something, give something, help someone, together we can make a difference.[20]

I invite you to pause with me right now. If you've encountered unkindness today, breathe in, then exhale any animosity you feel. If someone has been kind to you today, breathe in and thank God. Now let's all ask God the Holy Spirit to show us one specific way that we can show people God's heart of kindness today. Pray with me, dear one.

Jesus, You are the perfect example of kindness.
You are Almighty, yet You're also rich
in mercy and grace.
Thank You that Your kindness brings peace.
I want that for my world, Lord.
Would You please reveal one specific way I can
show Your kindness today? I'm listening and I
will follow Your Way. In Your name, amen.

Kindness Is a Choice

*He was very well respected—not just because he had
a college education and wore a shirt and tie every day
but because he was never condescending to people. He
was respectful and kind; and even though people in our
community called each other by their first names, my
dad remained Mr. Downey to many.*

BOX OF BUTTERFLIES

*Therefore, as God's chosen people, holy and dearly loved,
clothe yourselves with compassion, kindness, humility,
gentleness and patience.*

COLOSSIANS 3:12

My father was a thoughtful man, and I adored him. After my mother's death, I became more attached to him than ever. He was a schoolmaster, and later ran a mortgage-loan company. In a predominantly working-class neighborhood, my father's clothing stood out. But Dad clothed himself in more than professional attire. His heart was clothed with a humble and patient compassion that actively worked to help others. His acts of kindness spread far and wide.[21]

What do your clothes say about you, dear one?

Your physical clothing says something to the world, doesn't it?

Maybe it's, *Look at me!* Or, *Please* don't *look at me!* Maybe it's, *I'm going to work out any minute!* Or maybe I'm just speaking for a friend . . .

We usually think about our outfit for the day, but have you ever thought about how you dress your heart? For most people, this is a totally new concept; Colossians 3:12 commands all of us to consider this, though. My father clothed himself in compassion, kindness, humility, gentleness, and patience. Because my dad "dressed" this way, lives were changed.

How you and I dress our hearts determines how we act, too. If you're dressed in kindness, you'll act kindly. If you're dressed in bitterness, kindness won't be your first response.

I'm sure you see where I'm headed with this.

We can deliberately choose how to dress our hearts each day. By the grace of God, we can let go of resentment and choose compassion for others. In His power, we can lay down pride and put on humility. Instead of being sarcastic, we can clothe our words with gentleness. Rather than flipping out, we can stop, breathe, and respond with patience.

We can only do these things if we've chosen ahead of time to let God clothe us in His virtues. Can you imagine how the world might change if we all did this? Let's get dressed up in kindness, my friend!

Heavenly Father, thank You for
being kind, patient, and humble.
You give us the perfect example of how to love and live.
Thank You for every person who has shown us kindness.
It can be tough to choose compassion and gentleness
in this world.
Please clothe us in kindness so we can change the world for You.
We love You and trust You, Lord.
In Jesus' name, amen.

Kindness Builds Bridges

Peace Bridge opened over the River Foyle in 2011. But back in the 1970s, my dad encouraged me to explore how we each could be that bridge in our own lives.

BOX OF BUTTERFLIES

For God so loved the world that He gave His one and only Son, that whoever believes in Him shall not perish but have eternal life. For God did not send His Son into the world to condemn the world, but to save the world through Him.

JOHN 3:16–17

The River Foyle divides Derry City, the beautiful town where I grew up. As the Troubles escalated, the communities on either side of the river became more and more segregated. It broke my heart to see our town split in two. But my dad refused to give up hope. He always looked for ways to build bridges. He always spoke of tolerance and kindness. He taught me that we should reach out to each other in love.

It did not occur to me until I was an adult, growing in my own faith, just how like Jesus my father was. During the lengthy, turbulent, and often-painful time in our community, Dad taught me—through action and in word—that we need to have eyes to see and a heart open to each God-given opportunity to extend kindness to

51

others. He modeled so well the high calling of Christ to love rather than condemn, as John 3:16–17 describes.

Dad also helped me understand that kindness doesn't have to be loud or huge. Quiet by nature, he was prone to performing small acts of kindness. He believed love is a verb and he had a special way of showing love.

Instead of judging others, kindness chooses to see the best in people. Rather than condemning others, kindness operates on the principle of Grace; because of God's unconditional and undeserved blessing for us, we treat others as Jesus would treat them. And instead of separating us, kindness builds bridges that bring people together.

Dear one, is your life—what you say, post, and do—currently building bridges between people?

Just as it was easier during the Irish Troubles to tear others down rather than build them up, it's simpler today to steer clear of others and stay within our own "tribe," the people we enjoy and think like. If Jesus had acted in that way, though, He never would have come to earth. Our Heavenly Father sent Jesus to build bridges, and our call in Him is the same.

It may not be the easy path, but it is the Christlike one. Together, let's commit to staying on the path of kindness, building bridges, and spreading God's love.

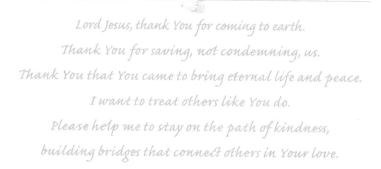

Lord Jesus, thank You for coming to earth.
Thank You for saving, not condemning, us.
Thank You that You came to bring eternal life and peace.
I want to treat others like You do.
Please help me to stay on the path of kindness,
building bridges that connect others in Your love.
In Your name, amen.

Kindness Creates Peace

*This area of the cemetery offered no protection. A wide,
lonely hillside on a cold afternoon. And here I was,
wearing a bright red cape.*

BOX OF BUTTERFLIES

*Get rid of all bitterness, rage, anger, harsh words, and
slander, as well as all types of evil behavior. Instead, be
kind to each other, tenderhearted, forgiving one another,
just as God through Christ has forgiven you.*

EPHESIANS 4:31–32

As children growing up in the Troubles, we would sometimes get detoured on our way home from school because
of bomb scares or gun battles. We learned from an early
age to hide behind cars and walls, quickly becoming little experts on
telling how close the gunfire was.[22]

Danger could come out of nowhere. And often it did.

Not long after my mother's passing, my auntie Ruby took me up
to the cemetery to visit my mom's grave. It was Mother's Day, and a
cold and damp wind blew sharply. I had bundled up in my favorite
red woolen cape, with fake fur trim, a shield against the sharp chill
in the air.

When the first gunshot rang out, Ruby and I dropped instinctively. But there was no protection on the hillside where my mother had been laid to rest, so Ruby pulled me to my feet again. We began to run. More gunfire split the air, and we saw others running for cover or dropping down behind gravestones for protection.

"Get down; get down where you are!" a man yelled, seeing my bright red cape and realizing how much of a target it made me. Ruby pulled me to the ground once again, just as we both smelled a scent like burnt hair. She covered me with her body as we lay on the cold, wet earth.

Finally, the shooting stopped, and we cautiously got up and embraced in gratitude. With my trembling hand tight in hers, Auntie Ruby hurried me back down the hill, toward the safety of home. Once inside I ran into my father's arms and started crying, and I remember he held me tenderly and, to calm me down, he began gently rubbing my back.

Suddenly he stopped. "Ruby, come look at this." There, on the fake fur trim of my hooded red cape, was a large singed hole where a bullet had narrowly missed my head.[23]

From that day forward, I had a choice to make.

Thanks to the Christlike example of my father, one of the kindest men who ever lived, I decided *against* bitterness and rage. Dad raised me to believe that kindness can change the world. So, instead of becoming resentful, I allowed growing up in such troubled times to plant in me a deep desire to spread peace and love in the world.

What about you? However you grew up, today is another day to choose. Will you work toward creating peace, one act of kindness at a time, or will you hold on to bitterness? I'd like to pray for us as we choose.

Lord, horrible things happen in this
broken world.
Children are hurt; wars rage;
Your people are divided.
But You have given us the power to
make a difference.
Please help us to choose kindness instead
of resentment and anger.
We need Your help, Lord.
And we ask for it in the name of Jesus.
Amen.

Kindness Changes Everything

They hear rumors about this medical group coming, a group of doctors who supposedly have the ability to fix faces. And a seed of hope is planted. This seed of hope drives mothers to walk miles or get on a bus to go to far-off places, all in hopes that their child might be given a chance at a normal life.

But the fruit of the Spirit is love, joy, peace, forbearance, kindness, goodness, faithfulness, gentleness and self-control . . .

It's been my great privilege to serve God alongside Operation Smile for many years. I first encountered this wonderful ministry while recording an episode for *Touched by an Angel* featuring a single mother, Ginger, who believed her bad choices caused her daughter's cleft palate. My angel-character, Monica, babysits Ginger's precious little girl, who hears from a neighbor that free surgeries are offered to help people like her.

I love that this episode speaks to the truth that, despite what Ginger believed, God does *not* punish us for our past (see Psalm 103:8–10). I also love that viewers were introduced to the real-life medical professionals of Operation Smile, who change lives around the globe by performing no-cost craniofacial surgeries for impoverished families.

Many children with cleft palates are born into cultures with profound stigmas, where craniofacial anomalies are viewed as a curse and shame on the family. The mothers of these children worry and struggle. They pray for a cure, not realizing that one exists.

When families meet the kind doctors and nurses of Operation Smile, seeds of hope grow. Tentative, yet trusting, a mother hands her child over to a medical team who often don't speak the same language as her. And then comes my favorite moment, not long after surgery, when mother and child reunite. The child, who that mother thought would never smile, who might never have had the chance at a normal life, smiles up at her for the first time. Joy and gratitude overflow while tears stream down every face. No words are needed. We all rejoice together in the power of healing, in the gift of second chances.[24]

It's a holy moment.

The kindness of complete strangers who travel, often thousands of miles, to perform surgeries overwhelms these families. And then, as mothers return home with healed children, the fruit of God's Spirit—love, joy, peace, and kindness—reverberates into entire communities. With Operation Smile, it's never only one life that changes. As it always does, kindness radiates outward, transforming everyone it touches.

Your daily acts of kindness reverberate through eternity, too. You may think, *I've never done anything big like that*, but *kindness is not measured in quantity but in quality*. Be on the lookout today for kindness opportunities. Be part, this day, of adding to the kindness radiating from God's heart to the world.

Heavenly Father, You are so kind to us,
Your beloved children.
Thank You for treating us, not as we deserve,
but with Your never-stopping,
never-giving-up, always-and-forever grace.
Your mercies are new this morning.
I want to show kindness.
Please help me to do that today.
In Jesus' name, amen.

Kindness Pays Attention

I've learned that people will forget what you said,
people will forget what you did, but people will never
forget how you made them feel.

MAYA ANGELOU

The Lord bless you
and keep you;
the Lord make His face shine on you
and be gracious to you;
the Lord turn His face toward you
and give you peace.

NUMBERS 6:24–26

Long before I had the pleasure of meeting Maya Angelou on set, I had admired her voice, literally and artistically. Meeting her in person did not disappoint. She was one of those people who you just know have much to say. When she spoke, you listened. Even so, she had the gift of giving people her full attention. When she turned her gaze on you, you felt truly seen and heard and recognized. She had an extraordinary gift for raising everyone up and making every single person feel very special. There was a presence about her—of greatness, of humility, of spirit.[25]

In today's age of perpetual distraction, one of the greatest gifts you can give another person is the gift of attention. What kindness we can show when we simply make and keep eye contact with someone!

I remember taking my daughter, Reilly, to meet Maya while she was on tour for her beautiful book of essays *Letter to My Daughter*. I will never forget how Maya looked at my daughter, with eyes full of love and a heart full of faith and promise. As busy as she was, Maya gave Reilly her full attention, breathing life into her through words of wisdom and kindness.

The Bible tells us that our Heavenly Father turns His face toward us, that He blesses us with grace and peace. What a stunningly beautiful thought! The God of the universe gives you His full attention. He looks on you with kindness and mercy.

He invites you to look on people in the same way, to give them your full attention, to leave them feeling fully seen, heard, and recognized. In a world where so many look on one another as competitors or conspirators, people who treat others with attentive kindness truly stand out.

You and I can best pass on kindness when we've first received it from our loving Heavenly Father. He is looking on you with kindness right this instant! You are His beloved child. Will you take a moment with me right now, close your eyes, and allow God's loving-kindness to fill you?

As you head into the rest of your day, look on others with kindness. Give them your full attention. They will never forget how you made them feel.

Father, what a gift Your loving attention is.
You are so kind to us.
You don't look on us to judge, but to bless
with grace and peace.
Thank You.
Please help me to treat others the same way—
with so much kindness that they go away
feeling as special
as You made them to be.
In Jesus' name, amen.

When you play an angel on TV, people begin to think you are an angel in real life.

BOX OF BUTTERFLIES

She opens her mouth with wisdom, and the teaching of kindness is on her tongue.

PROVERBS 31:26, ESV

I'm the first person to tell you that I am just as flawed as everyone else, that I am far from perfect. But playing an angel for almost ten years not only had a positive influence on the audience; it had a huge impact on me as well. I began to realize that we all have the opportunity to be an angel—a messenger of God—if we are just willing to show kindness and grace to those around us.

While filming *Touched by an Angel*, I often went to Salt Lake City's Primary Children's Hospital to visit families facing serious illnesses. One day, around Christmas, I was there, wearing a Santa hat and bringing a festive spirit to those sequestered in the hospital. As I walked down the corridor, I saw a family exiting one of the rooms.

There was no question what they had just experienced. You could feel the grief gust like wind out of their room. The mother, looking up, saw me and gasped. Rushing over and grabbing my hands, she exclaimed, "Oh, Monica! I prayed that an angel would come for my baby. And here you are! Here you are."

I silently held this woman while she cried. I prayed quietly with her. I prayed with all my heart. After a few moments, she pulled back and looked me in the eyes. "Thank you; that was just what I needed."

She left, but I stood there, overwhelmed with emotion.

Monica was the name of the angel I played on television, but *I* wasn't Monica; I was just Roma. I called Della later that evening, distressed and confused. "I didn't know what to say," I cried.

"Baby, I don't understand what you're so upset about. You did the right thing."

I tried to explain again. "Della, she thought God had sent an angel to her."

To which Della replied, "And who said He didn't?"

The dictionary defines "angel" as "a spiritual being that serves, especially as a messenger from God." We are all spiritual beings, and we all have the ability to be messengers of God.[26]

What message are you regularly sending with your words? Proverbs 31 teaches that a person of excellence speaks words of wisdom and kindness. Could the words you speak every day be categorized in this way? Let us all pray to use kinder and wiser words from this day forward.

Heavenly Father, thank You for the chance
to be messengers of Your love and truth.
Thank You that Your Word, the Bible, is full
of loving-kindness.
Please help me to choose words of kindness and wisdom.
Please forgive me for the times I've spoken
unkindly and foolishly.
Make me more like You, Lord.
In Jesus' name I pray, amen.

Courage

The Courage to Be Generous

*The only thing they asked was that I pay the kindness
forward with my life. And I have tried to do that over
the years to honor their generosity.*

BOX OF BUTTERFLIES

*Remember this: Whoever sows sparingly will also reap
sparingly, and whoever sows generously will also reap
generously. Each of you should give what you have
decided in your heart to give, not reluctantly or under
compulsion, for God loves a cheerful giver. And God
is able to bless you abundantly, so that in all things at
all times, having all that you need, you will abound in
every good work.*

2 CORINTHIANS 9:7–8

Years ago, the courageous generosity of three people changed
the course of my life.

I had secured a position at the prestigious Drama Studio in London. Thrilled about the quality of training I would receive, but knowing I couldn't afford the cost of tuition on my own, I applied for a grant. My heart sank when I was turned down.

While I was trying to process my disappointment, a miracle occurred. Three extraordinary people whom I had worked with on a summer theater project banded together and offered to put up the money for me to attend. They told me they believed in me and wanted to invest in my future. It wasn't a loan, they assured me; it was an investment in me.

I had never experienced such unbelievable, unselfish kindness. But before I could accept, I told them I had to talk it over with my father. My dad was stunned. Of course he wished he could pay the tuition himself, but it was more than our family could afford. Knowing this was an incredible opportunity for me, he said he couldn't let pride stand in the way and he gave me permission to accept.[27]

These wonderful, generous friends gave me so much more than financial assistance. They gave me confidence and encouragement. The word "encouragement" literally means to "embolden with courage," and that's precisely what I received from these three angel friends.

I read verses like the ones from 2 Corinthians 9 and I can't help but think about the generosity that changed my life. Imagine if my friends had sown "sparingly." *I may need that money for something else*, they could have thought. Or, *What if she misuses the funds?* They could have given reluctantly. Instead, these amazing friends gave cheerfully.

I love that, through passages like 2 Corinthians 9, our Heavenly Father promises that, if we are courageously generous, He will take care of our needs . . . abundantly! Jesus is lovingly inviting you to be generous today. How will you respond?

Heavenly Father, You are so generous to us.
Every day You pour out Your
amazing blessings.
Help me to be like You, Lord,
generous and kind.
Help me to give courageously, not reluctantly.
You can be trusted with everything,
including the resources that You've
provided me and others.
May others know more of Your love through me.
In Jesus' name, amen.

The Courage to Step Out

I was scared, of course. The unknown opened up before me.
But when nothing is certain, everything is possible.

BOX OF BUTTERFLIES

". . . if you can do anything, take pity on us and help us."
" 'If you can'?" said Jesus. "Everything is possible for
one who believes."
Immediately the boy's father exclaimed,
"I do believe; help me overcome my unbelief!"

MARK 9:22B-24

After graduating from drama school in London, some of my friends planned to move to New York. We were trained and ready and eager to start our professional lives. I knew it would require a big leap of faith to move thousands of miles away, but I was a young woman with a big dream. I prayed I would know what direction to take, that God would guide me to each next step, and that I would have the courage to take it.[28]

It was unnerving. I was unsure. But when nothing is certain, everything is possible.

It takes a special kind of courage to step out when there are no guarantees. I'm so grateful that God gives us this kind of courage when we need it most. My move to New York required courage in the face of uncertainty, but God promises to give us courage when we need it, regardless of the circumstance.

Mark 9 tells the story of a beleaguered and frightened father who brings his son to Jesus' disciples. Watching his son be tormented for many years must have been impossibly difficult for this father. Sadly, the disciples cannot help the boy. Uncertainty—perhaps even hopelessness—hangs heavy in the air. Then Jesus arrives on the scene. Everything is about to change.

The father begs Jesus to help. ". . . if you can do anything . . . ," he pleads.

Jesus responds with a life-changing truth: "Everything is possible for one who believes."

Wow! It's a breathtaking promise.

Everything is possible for one who believes.

Do you believe it?

I love the example of the father in Mark 9, who vulnerably admits, "I do believe; help me overcome my unbelief" (verse 24). He believed; he also needed Jesus' help to overcome every shred of insecurity threatening his confidence in God. If we're willing to admit it, I think we all need that help.

What seems impossible to you today? What do you need courage to face?

It may be something exciting but intimidating, as I faced in moving to New York to begin my professional career. It may be something as heartbreaking as a loved one's lengthy illness. Whatever you're facing, I encourage you today to respond to Jesus with words of decision and humble hope: "I do believe; help me overcome my unbelief."

Thank You, Jesus, for Your miracle-working power.
Thank You that nothing is too difficult for You.
Thank You for the promise that
nothing is impossible for those who believe.
I choose to believe You today.
Please help me in my unbelief.
Help me to choose trust and confidence in You.
I love You, Lord.
Amen.

The Courage to Be Vulnerable

There are often hundreds of actors pursuing a single role. And the truth is that you could give the audition of your life, and they still might reject you just because of the color of your hair or because you're too different from how directors envision the character.

BOX OF BUTTERFLIES

"My grace is sufficient for you, for My power is made perfect in weakness."

2 CORINTHIANS 12:9

To survive in the entertainment industry, you must learn to live with fear.

Rosalind Russell, an actress from the 1930s until the '70s, once said, "Acting is standing up naked and turning around very slowly." Of course, she was speaking about being emotionally naked, about appearing vulnerable in front of others. Actors must learn to not only live with the fear of being vulnerable; they must conquer it.

I don't know anyone who *likes* being vulnerable and afraid. Most people actively avoid situations that leave them feeling exposed.

For an actress, however, fear of failure and rejection is simply part of the territory. I learned quite early on that developing a thick skin and the motivation to continue even in the face of disappointments, setbacks, and rejections was necessary. Because I'm naturally a sensitive, tenderhearted person, thick skin didn't come naturally to me. I had to cultivate the strength *not* to take rejection to heart.

Relying on God, not on my performance or my resumé, was key.

Whether you're an actress or an accountant, a mother, manicurist, or marine biologist, what you do—and how successful you are at doing it—never tells the whole story. If life is all "up to us," we're sunk. Thankfully, life *isn't* up to us; but it takes great courage to acknowledge we are vulnerable, that we need God, that we can't do life on our own. Only God's all-sufficient strength can transform fear of failure into faith.

In 2 Corinthians 12, the Apostle Paul details his deliberate choice to set aside his successes and failures to focus on Jesus instead. Paul invites us to trade our weaknesses and fears for God's strength and sufficiency.

Acting required me to develop a thick skin, but life requires all of us to develop something greater: unshakable faith in God.

Where is your faith today? Whose strength are you currently relying on, my friend? Are you trying to face life on your own or are you trusting the sufficiency of Christ? Are you judging yourself by what you do or are you confident in Whose you are? Will you pray with me about this?

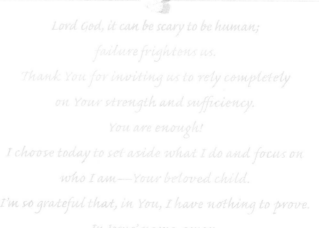

Lord God, it can be scary to be human;
failure frightens us.
Thank You for inviting us to rely completely
on Your strength and sufficiency.
You are enough!
I choose today to set aside what I do and focus on
who I am—Your beloved child.
I'm so grateful that, in You, I have nothing to prove.
In Jesus' name, amen.

The Courage to Overcome

*No matter what your profession, we all face "those" feelings sometimes.
Feelings of unworthiness. Feelings of failure. Feelings of defeat.*

BOX OF BUTTERFLIES

*This is My command—be strong and courageous! Do
not be afraid or discouraged. For the Lord your God is
with you wherever you go.*

JOSHUA 1:9, NLT

Because God has granted me a wonderful measure of success, some people believe I've never dealt with negative thoughts and doubts about my abilities. That simply isn't true. No matter what we do or who we are, all humans face feelings of failure, defeat, and unworthiness at some point. We're all in the same boat!

But we don't have to stay in that boat. I have found that the best remedy to negative thoughts is to move myself from a place of fear into a space of love.

In the classic movie musical *The Sound of Music*, actress Julie Andrews gives courage to the von Trapp children during a storm. Do you remember how she did it? She urges them to think of a few of their favorite things. That's a version of what I try to do. I start by simply thinking about the people I love. I count my blessings, I pray, and I connect to God. Then I am reminded that God has a plan for my life, even when I cannot clearly see it.

The time I spend in that space of love with God restores me and gives me courage and joy; my sense of purpose rises again. I am filled back up so that I can go out into the world and chase my dreams, energized, excited, and full of faith.[29]

In Joshua 1:9, Moses reminds his young general that God is with him wherever he goes. That promise is for you and me as surely as it was for Joshua and Moses. God will never leave us or forsake us. Never! Because of this, we can be courageous and strong.

The next time you hear negative messages, I invite you to move out of that space and into courageous love. Start by counting your blessings. Pray. Connect to God. He will remind you of His plan and purpose for your life. Jeremiah 29:11 promises that His plans for you are good, that He will give you hope and a future.

Knowing that God is *for us* and *with us* gives us courage. It helps us face down fears and doubts with His strength. Today, my friend, let's be strong and courageous, trusting God and rejecting negative self-talk. I have no doubt that we'll be glad we did!

Thank You, Lord, for promising to be with us . . .

always.

We are so grateful for Your faithfulness.

Thank You for empowering us to face our fears.

In Your strength, we can overcome negative self-talk.

You tell us that we are beloved, valuable, and

made for a glorious purpose.

Please help us to trust You in this.

We love You!

Amen.

The Courage to Be Ready

*I spent several years in New York trying to make
things happen. I booked some regional theater shows,
which were good experiences but did not pay much.
In between shows, I went to acting classes and exercise
classes, making sure that I was ready.*

BOX OF BUTTERFLIES

*Be on your guard; stand firm in the faith;
be courageous; be strong.
Do everything in love.*

1 CORINTHIANS 16:13–14

An acting teacher of mine always said that if opportunity knocks, it needs to find you ready and prepared, not taking a nap on the couch.[30] To this day, that's some of the best counsel I've ever been given.

Being ready requires commitment. Staying ready means working when it would be easier to relax. Being prepared means training when there's no game or job on the line. Sometimes it means working hard when there aren't even any prospects. Courage is required to remain ready, trusting that something will come.

The Apostle Paul closed his first letter to the Corinthian church with words of encouragement. He wanted them to be ready, come what may. He wanted them to be strong, courageous, and loving . . . all at the same time. He wanted them to stand firm in their convictions, unwaveringly committed to God.

These are important words for people of faith today. We need to be ready professionally, to honor God with the gifts, talents, and opportunities He's given us. And we need to be ready in our faith, firmly grounded in the truth of God's Word. In all of this, we need to *do everything in love.*

Challenging? Certainly. Nonnegotiable? Absolutely.

For believers, love must be the foundation under and the seal over all that we do. We may be prepared to defend our convictions, but doing so without love makes us "like a resounding gong or a clanging cymbal" (1 Corinthians 13:1). We can be prepared for every professional possibility but be unloving in our ambition. Stepping on people in our attempt to climb the ladder doesn't just hurt others; it diminishes us. It takes courage to be kind and humble in the professional arena, but this is the path of love.

As people of faith, we are invited to courageously work hard. To exert effort. To develop readiness and alertness in what we do, say, and believe. And, in all of life, we are called to choose love.

Please take a moment with me and pray. God may desire to make you ready for something. He may ask you to prepare for some future purpose you can't yet see. When opportunity comes knocking, will you be ready?

Lord God, thank You for preparing us.
We don't have to figure everything out on our own.
I am so thankful for that!
You are good and kind.
You give us courage to work hard
and be prepared,
no matter what might come our way.
Please help us to do everything with love,
just like Your Word commands.
In Jesus' name, amen.

The Courage to Check Pride

*I would check people's coats, sit and read for a few hours
while they dined, and then retrieve their coats for them
around ten or eleven.*

BOX OF BUTTERFLIES

*Before a downfall the heart is haughty,
but humility comes before honor.*

PROVERBS 18:12

Humility goes against almost every human instinct. We want to be noticed and honored, not overlooked and unappreciated. Most people want to be handing their coat to someone else, not be the person cheerfully taking the coat at the check station. Humility actually requires great courage.

I had been classically trained at an elite London theater school. At graduation, I received the Most Promising Student of the Year award. I could have refused to work hard and be patient, believing I was too good to check coats. But I had been raised with shining examples of hard work and humility. I thank God for that.

Each night, as I arrived at the fancy Upper West Side restaurant to take my position as the coat-check girl, I brought a book and a willing heart. I treated people with the kindness I had been raised to value.

One evening, a popular talk show host, Regis Philbin, walked up and asked what I was reading. We chatted for a few moments, and he noticed my Irish accent. I took his coat, and he enjoyed dinner with his lovely wife. He treated me with kindness, even leaving me a twenty-dollar tip. His generosity encouraged me tremendously.

Many years later, when I appeared on his talk show, doing publicity for *Touched by an Angel*, I retold this story. I had been in a position of humility at the coat-check stand; now I was in a position of honor. What a wild turn of events!

The Bible tells us that humility comes before honor. Pride gets in the way of our calling and only leads to harm. I realize this goes against what the world teaches, but humility really is the path of life. You can only enjoy the honor you receive if God has set you free of the pride that poisons it.

You may be in a place that feels low today. You may be changing diapers or checking coats. You may feel your ship has sailed or your time has passed. Take heart, dear one. Be courageous! God sees every humble heart and honors the hard work it takes to stay the course. He is proud of every person who chooses to treat others with humble kindness rather than haughty resentment.

Take a moment and breathe deeply with Jesus. Entrust your heart to Him, however humble or honored your current circumstances might be. With God is the path of life and peace.

Lord God, I don't know where the people reading
this book are at today, but You do.
You know whether they feel high or low.
You know that our world prizes pride,
not humility.
But You lived with humility, gentleness,
and kindness
when You walked on earth.
Please help us to walk like You.
We love you and trust You.
In Jesus' name, amen.

The Courage to Move Forward

Nothing gets going from a stationary position. Energy
begets energy; one thing leads to another. Each step of
my journey opened the door for the next step.

BOX OF BUTTERFLIES

Whether you turn to the right or to the left, your ears will hear a
voice behind you, saying, "This is the way; walk in it."

ISAIAH 30:21

My coat checking gave way to some acting work, and I was
finally cast Off-Broadway, at New York's Public Theater
and the Roundabout Theatre. I was thrilled to be doing
what I was trained for and what I loved. It wasn't Broadway yet, but
it was interesting, quality work, and it paid, supplementing my other
part-time gigs.

Sometimes we say no to opportunities because they may not be
exactly what we are looking for. But the truth is you never know
where things might lead. You've got to stay open and have faith.

Giving my all and working hard Off-Broadway led to being noticed by Sir Rex Harrison, an Academy– and Tony–Award-winning
actor mounting a production of W. Somerset Maugham's *The Circle*
for Broadway. I nearly fainted when Sir Rex, in his impeccably tai-
lored suit, walked into my dressing room and asked me to audition
for one of the lead roles. Of course, I said yes!

Landing that role led to performing alongside two other old-time movie stars, Glynis Johns and Stewart Granger. The wisdom and stories of experience I heard from my co-stars shaped me in profound ways. It also led to an exhilarating six-month Broadway run. I will never forget that first performance on the Broadway stage in New York. Taking my bow at curtain call, I was overcome with emotion.[31]

And I could have missed it all.

I could have said no to each "small" part I had been offered. I could have turned up my nose at the idea of checking coats for people in "the business." I could have been too intimidated to audition for a role alongside Sir Rex Harrison. But think how much I would have missed!

I recognize it takes courage to get going and to move forward, especially when what you hope for or dream about seems so far off. I love that, through His Word, God infuses us with confidence. Isaiah 30:21 empowers us to take steps with courage, knowing God will guide us. We can trust Him.

Isaiah 30:21 is a call to trust and listen; it's also a call to obedience. We cannot simply wait around for God's will to drop into our laps. We must courageously move forward as He leads.

Where might God be leading you today, dear one? Together, let's ask and listen for our next, best step.

Heavenly Father, thank You for guiding us.
Thank You for making Your way known.
You have given us Your Word and Your Spirit lives in us.
We can listen to and trust You, Lord.
Please help us obey You and courageously move forward.
Please show us the next, best step.
In Jesus' name, amen.

The Courage to Get Out of the Boat

Living a life of faith means learning to get our feet wet.

BOX OF BUTTERFLIES

"Lord, if it's You," Peter replied, "tell me to come to You on the water."
"Come," Jesus said.

MATTHEW 14:28-29

Some Bible stories never fail to amaze me. The account of Jesus walking on water—and inviting His disciple Peter to join Him—definitely falls into that category. Can you imagine?

Matthew 14 tells us that, after preaching to a large crowd, Jesus made His disciples get in a boat while He went up on a mountainside by Himself to pray. According to verse 24, the disciples sailed "a considerable distance from land, buffeted by the waves."

Storms on the Sea of Galilee are no laughing matter. Winds can create waves up to ten feet high, more than capable of capsizing wooden vessels like the ones in which Jesus' disciples would have sailed.

Put yourself in their position for just a moment. How frightening to sail in such conditions! Then imagine the shock of seeing Jesus walking toward you . . . *walking on water.* Understandably, "they were terrified" (14:26).

"But Jesus immediately said to them: 'Take courage! It is I. Don't be afraid'" (14:27).

What happens next inspires me tremendously.

Peter asks to be invited out. Jesus told all the disciples to take courage, but only one acted on it. "Peter got down, walked on the water and came toward Jesus" (14:29). True, when he looked down at the wind and waves, Peter began to sink. But as soon as he cried out, "immediately Jesus reached out His hand and caught him" (14:30).

I've heard it said that the only difference between excitement and fear is your attitude. An attitude of courage leads to incredible experience. Fear, on the other hand, keeps you in the boat. I love that, through this story, we also see that courage and sinking aren't mutually exclusive. Even if we've stepped out in faith and the storm gets the better of us, Jesus is right there to save.

I don't know about you, but I would rather walk a few steps on water than sit in the boat. I want to courageously trust, looking only at Jesus. How about you?

After Jesus saved Peter and climbed into the boat with him, the wind died down. And all the disciples worshiped Jesus, "saying, 'Truly You are the Son of God'" (14:33). Walking in courage leads to worship. Having Jesus in the boat leads to peace. Let's thank and worship Him today, asking for the courage to get our feet wet in faith.

Jesus, thank You for telling us we don't have to be afraid.

Thank You for Peter's example of courageous faith.

Please help us to trust You so much that we get out of the boat.

We worship You today. You are worthy of all praise!

You are the Son of God.

Thank You for coming to earth in love, grace, and truth.

In Your name we pray, amen.

The Courage to Be Noisy

At the National Prayer Breakfast, to an audience of leaders
from around the world, Mark and I described what it felt
like to be called "the noisiest Christians in Hollywood."

BOX OF BUTTERFLIES

I am not ashamed of the Gospel, because it is the power of
God that brings salvation to everyone who believes . . .

ROMANS 1:16

I n bringing the Bible to television, Mark and I knew we'd face critics in Hollywood, a place known for unfriendliness to the Gospel message. Fielding criticism from entertainment professionals was expected; grappling with friends who also tried to dissuade us was not.

People thought we were nuts. "It's too risky, too big." "What if you get it wrong?" "You can't win; you will fail." "No one cares about the Bible anymore." "No one will buy it in Hollywood." "It could be a noisy, humiliating flop!"

We heard their concerns and didn't necessarily disagree with them. But instead of bowing to fear, we stepped out with courage. We called in prayer and moved forward in faith. We chose to listen to the Spirit's positive whisper of encouragement rather than the negative messages of the world.[32]

Like Paul, the author of Romans 1:16, Mark and I have chosen not to be ashamed of our faith. We know that being identified as "the noisiest Christians in Hollywood" comes with great risk and great responsibility. Courage is required.

How easy is it for you to be courageous in sharing your faith, my friend?

It can be hard, can't it? If I'm not careful, I can let negative messages creep in: *It's too risky. What if I get it wrong? I might look foolish. They'll reject me. No one cares about God or the Bible anymore.* Maybe you've been there, thought that?

It takes courage to speak out for Jesus. Remember, courage is not the absence of fear. You may still experience fear, but courage enables you to move forward anyway. And in this case, the reward was so worth it. When Mark and I stepped out in faith, incredible things happened. Things only God could make happen. The *Bible* miniseries was so much bigger than us—bigger than we could ever have imagined—and it was God's work. We just needed the courage to be noisy for Christ.

Would you like to have that courage? It's yours for the taking!

One caveat: I'm not encouraging you to be noisy in an unkind way. Quite the opposite. We're called to be like Jesus, speaking truth *in love*. It doesn't take a ton of courage to digitally yell at someone on social media. But being lovingly loud for Jesus does. I am praying you'll have the courage to live loud in love today.

Lord, equip me to speak the truth in love,
helping others to know You.
Thank You that all of us get to be
part of Your work.
Please help us know how to use our gifts
and talents for You.
May we be noisy in the right way, God . . .
in Your Way . . .
that people might receive Your love
and everlasting life.
For Jesus' sake, amen.

The Courage to Wait

*We were just weeks from beginning principal
photography, and we had not yet cast our most
important role: Jesus.
To say this made us nervous would be an
understatement.*

BOX OF BUTTERFLIES

*Lead me in Your truth and teach me, for You are the
God of my salvation; for You I wait all the day long.*

PSALM 25:5, ESV

Waiting can feel so impossibly difficult, can't it? Especially when you've courageously stepped out in faith but don't have all you need to move forward.

When Mark and I began developing the *Bible* project for the History channel, we knew God had called us to and equipped us for the endeavor. We stepped out bravely. But we needed an actor to play Jesus, and we simply couldn't find him.

Obviously, it takes a special actor to portray Jesus, Who is so much more than a character or historical figure. This person must have the special presence to depict someone both human and divine. In addition, he must be ready and willing to take on the role, which would be both daunting and difficult.

After weeks of praying fervently and emailing friends and church circles with the subject line "Looking for Jesus," I surrendered to God. I waited for Him. Everything in me wanted this settled; waiting was the last thing I wanted to do. But sometimes God asks us to step out in courage and sometimes He asks us to wait courageously. Only staying close to God in prayer helps us discern when to act and when to wait.

The still, small voice of God's Holy Spirit eventually spoke to me. Through a remarkable series of "coincidences," I received a recording of Portuguese actor Diogo Morgado reading on-camera. It got my attention right away, and God prompted me to follow up.

Miraculously, Diogo happened to be in Los Angeles and arrived at our home office the next day to discuss the project. We have glass on our front door, so we were able to peek out as Diogo walked up the path to our house. As he approached, a huge monarch butterfly the size of a small bird swooped down in front of his face, almost knocking him off his feet. If there had been any doubt in my mind before, it was instantly gone. God gave me a sign and He gave us our Jesus.

In Psalm 25:5 David declares, "for You I wait all the day long." The Hebrew word for "wait" here can also be translated "to wrap around" or "entwine." When God asks us to courageously wait, He's also inviting us to entwine ourselves more closely with Him than ever. Waiting wasn't easy, but I learned a special kind of courage through this experience. I pray that for you, too.

Thank You, Jesus, that when we look for You,
we find You.
We are so grateful for Your presence in our life.
Thank You, Holy Spirit, for teaching us
when to wait and when to step out.
Please grant us the courage to do whichever
You ask us to do.
We love You, Lord.
Amen.

The Courage to Surrender

*Abraham's faith shines through this story. He reassures
Isaac, "God Himself will provide the lamb for the
burnt offering." Somehow a substitute will be provided.
Somehow everything will be okay. Abraham knows that
Isaac is the promised one, so whatever happens, Isaac
will make it through. Abraham has a
resurrection-shaped faith.*

ADAPTED FROM ENGLISH THEOLOGIAN GLEN SCRIVENER

*The next day John saw Jesus coming toward him and said,
"Look, the Lamb of God, Who takes away the sin
of the world!"*

JOHN 1:29

Mark and I spent a great deal of time deciding which Old
Testament stories to include in *The Bible* miniseries. The
Old Testament spans so many years and has countless
characters. There were obviously some stories we knew we had to
incorporate, and then we had a wish list of others we thought might
work well on the screen.[33]

One of the stories we knew we needed to include is the account
of Abraham's courageous sacrifice in Genesis 22, which is one of
the most powerful and dramatic scenes in the Bible. Abraham is so

faithful that he is willing to surrender his only son, the son he and Sarah had prayed for, longed for, and whom God finally gave them in their old age. Abraham bravely trusts the Lord; and even though his heart is breaking, he does not question God and is prepared to do as He asks.

Mercifully, the angel of the Lord intervenes and says, "Do not lay a hand on the boy . . . Do not do anything to him. Now I know that you fear God, because you have not withheld from Me your son, your only son" (Genesis 22:12).

Consider for a moment the incredible courage it takes to sacrifice what you hold most dear. Through His Word, our Heavenly Father reveals that our brave sacrifices are safe in His hands. He provides all that we need when we surrender to Him. John 1:29 reveals that God also provided the perfect sacrifice to free us from the sin that so easily entangles: Jesus, the Lamb of God.

That's why Mark and I used the beautiful piece of music Hans Zimmer wrote for both the scene when Abraham courageously carried the wood for the sacrifice up Mount Moriah and when Jesus carried the wooden cross on which He would be sacrificed at Calvary.[34]

Very few of us will be asked by God, like Abraham was, to surrender *everything*. All of us are invited by God to sacrifice something. It's costly. It's sometimes confusing. It's always worth it.

I don't know where this devotional finds you today. You may feel that what God is calling you to lay down will cost you too much. Beloved one, my heart hurts with you. Wherever you are in your life, know that I am trusting God alongside you. We can walk with courage, knowing that God Himself withheld nothing to love us, but sacrificed His life that we might live.

Thank You, Jesus, for sacrificing Your life for us.
Your love sets us free.
We can never thank You enough.
It can be so scary to sacrifice, Lord.
Please help us to be courageous
like Abraham was,
willing to lay everything down because
he trusted You.
I choose to trust You today.
In Jesus' name, amen.

The Courage to Be Flexible

*In the middle of this arid desert, where we were trying
to create this series to honor God and His story,
I was the one who needed this reminder:*
I'm here with you. I'm carrying you. You are
never alone.

BOX OF BUTTERFLIES

We can make our plans, but the Lord determines our steps.

PROVERBS 16:9, NLT

Years ago, my daddy shared with me the "Footprints" poem. I found the words so comforting. It reminds me that even if we *feel* alone, we are *not* alone; the Lord carries us in His arms. I try to always keep a few credit–card–sized copies of "Footprints" in my wallet to share, in case I meet someone who needs encouragement. When I was headed to Morocco to film *The Bible* miniseries, I packed up a small bag to take on set with me. I felt a strong urge to include a "Footprints" card from my wallet. Someone might need it during filming.

Turns out someone did, and that someone was me.

We were filming the scene depicting Abraham's willingness to sacrifice his son and I had requested two white lambs for the scene. I've learned you always need a backup animal in case the first one doesn't cooperate. When the animal handler showed up on the day of filming, he brought two lambs as requested. But one was black and the other looked more like a muddy-colored goat.

Not what I expected.

I was upset and incredibly frustrated, compounded by the fact that we were at the summit of a remote mountaintop, not immediately close to anywhere. Getting a replacement lamb would cost time we simply didn't have. Some of my crew wondered why the color of the lamb was even important, but I knew that—to help our viewers make the connection between Abraham's sacrifice and Jesus as the Lamb of God sacrificed for us—we needed a symbol of purity and holiness.

I walked off the set, instantly aware that if I didn't take a moment to breathe and pray, I would cry. I reached into my purse to grab a tissue, and the "Footprints" poem fell out. I read it for the thousandth time, and God reminded me that He was near. He was carrying me. He would give me all I needed.

I walked forward with inspiration from His Spirit; He helped me exercise courageous flexibility. We would shoot the scene with the muddy-colored lamb and use special effects to change his color in postproduction. It would require time and creativity, but it was possible. All we needed was possible.

It takes courage to do difficult things; it also takes courage to be flexible when we've made plans. Remembering that God is with us, even when our plans get sidetracked, enables us to be brave and move forward on His path. As Proverbs 16 reminds us, "We can make our plans, but the Lord determines our steps." Whatever twists and turns your path takes today, remember that you *never* walk alone.

Thank You for encouraging us when
we need it most, Lord.
Thank You for never leaving us.
Thank You for Your good plans for us.
Please help us to be brave and flexible so we can
stay in step with You.
We trust You and Your plan.
We love You with all we are.
In Jesus' name, amen.

The Courage to Change

In my industry, you can be recognized as one of People
magazine's *"Most Beautiful People in the World" one
year, and the next year get no public attention at all.*

BOX OF BUTTERFLIES

*Even to your old age and gray hairs I am He, I am He
Who will sustain you. I have made you and I will carry
you; I will sustain you and I will rescue you.*

ISAIAH 46:4

Not too long ago, I celebrated one of those birthdays. You
know, the ones with a "zero" in it. My daughter, Reilly,
teased me affectionately, "It's just a birthday, Mom. But it
is a *big* one."

From our culture's standpoint, it certainly was. And in my line of
work, the kind of birthday I celebrated can feel downright terrifying.
The entertainment industry turns youth and a very particular kind
of beauty into idols that demand time and attention, not to mention
a small army of stylists and beauticians to maintain.

I'm so thankful that God has been my anchor in a business that's
obsessed with things that fade, no matter how hard we try. How my
skin looks and feels, how my body wrinkles, what I'm able to accom-
plish with the hours each day . . . all of this changes with age.

And I've learned to be at peace with this, dear one.

Of course, it can be challenging to see ourselves change. Some days vanity wants to get the better of me! Letting go of how we see ourselves, remembering how we used to be, can leave us feeling anxious and insecure.

It doesn't have to, however. We have a choice. We always have a choice.

Instead of cultivating the fear of letting go, I'm choosing to let go of fear.

The only way I'm able to do this is by staying closely connected with my Heavenly Father. He loves me whether my skin is smooth or not. He loves me no matter how my body changes. His love gives me the courage and strength I need to let go of my fear.

He loves you this way, too. No conditions. No limits.

Every moment, love flows from His heart to you, His beloved child.

Isaiah 46:4 promises that—even when our hair is white with age—God will be with us. He will sustain us, carry us, and rescue us. When we are troubled or too tired for the journey, He lovingly carries us in His arms. H sustains us with His strength, power, and peace and gives us the courage to go on.

We don't have to be afraid of letting go; let's choose to let go of fear instead.

Heavenly Father, thank You for your amazing promises.
I know You will carry me, sustain me, and help me,
no matter how old I get.
Thank You!
Please help me let go of fear and trust You more.
In Jesus' name, amen.

The Courage to Spend It All

When I stand before God at the end of my life, I would
hope that I would not have a single bit of talent left, and
could say, "I used everything You gave me."

ERMA BOMBECK

And whatever you do, whether in word or deed, do it all
in the name of the Lord Jesus, giving thanks to God the
Father through Him.

COLOSSIANS 3:17

After a spectacular victory, you may hear a professional athlete, while interviewed by a sportscaster, say something like "I knew I had to leave it all on the field." Artists express similar sentiments. Groundbreaking actor Michael Chekhov described it this way: This "is what you must give from the stage. Your life. No less. That is art: to give all you have."[35]

Give it all. Hold nothing back. Use everything God's given you.

How does this strike you?

Do you feel a thrill of anticipation or dread in the pit of your stomach?

Either way, I understand.

It takes a lot of courage to give everything. Only knowing that we are called to this by a loving Father, Who has equipped us for "every good work" (2 Timothy 3:17), empowers us fully. We aren't asked to give more than we've been given. We aren't asked to figure it out on our own. We're not judged or scolded. We are lovingly invited by our Heavenly Father to drink every drop of this beautiful life He's given us.

At the end of her life, Erma Bombeck wanted to stand before God with the confidence that she had used everything He had given her. I find that so inspiring. I want the same. And I want it, not just for me, but for you, too.

This life isn't meant to be carefully measured out, to be lived in safe and controlled ways. Jesus declared that He came to bring abundant life (John 10:10). Or, as Dallas Willard translated Jesus' words, "I have come into their world that they may have life, and life to the limit." Life to the limit, life without lack.[36]

Doesn't that sound amazing?

Would you take a moment with me and pray that we can live courageously and abundantly for God's glory?

Heavenly Father, thank You for giving us life.

You've given us more and better life than we could grasp for ourselves.

We are so grateful.

Please help us to be brave and to give everything for Your glory.

We are here for You, Lord, and we love You . . . always.

In Jesus' name, amen.

Love

Love Gives You Wings

When I think of my father, I can see that throughout my life, he was always trying to give me wings so that I could go anywhere I wanted . . . He was always supportive and encouraging of my artistic desires, and when the time came to interview for college, he went with me and sat in the waiting area.

BOX OF BUTTERFLIES

Those who hope in the Lord will renew their strength. They will soar on wings like eagles; they will run and not grow weary, they will walk and not be faint.

ISAIAH 40:31

My father truly was a remarkable man. After my mother passed, he learned to braid my hair. He took me shopping for dresses. He never wanted me to feel the void that was obviously there from us missing Mom. Bless him, he strove so hard to make things okay.[37]

As I grew older and prepared to leave Ireland for theater school in England, I began to feel anxious. Remember, this is before the Internet and cell phones! Being away from my father, with no way of immediately reaching him, made me extremely nervous.

One night, just a few days before I was scheduled to leave, he took me outside. It was a clear night with a full moon. And he said, "Roma, wherever you are in the world, that moon will be shining on you. So whenever you feel alone, always look into the night sky, and you'll be reminded of how much I love you. I'll leave a message for you in the moon."

As the first full moon ascended after I had settled in England, I went outside and looked up at it. I felt my dad's love and it was a great comfort.[38]

The message of my father's love, repeated over and over, gave me wings to soar.

What joy to discover that my Heavenly Father sends the same message to me. He sends the same message to you. If we hope in the Lord, Isaiah 40:31 promises, He will renew our strength. He will give us the wings of eagles, the strength to keep running on this often-difficult road of life. In good times and bad, He empowers us to keep walking.

I was blessed to have an earthly father who made this message clear. My heart grieves for those who did not hear, from their earthly fathers, that they are loved, that they have wings to soar.

Wherever we came from, all of us can hear today, from our Heavenly Father—whose opinion is infinitely and eternally more important—that we *can* and *will* soar when we trust in Him. His love never fails. Let's pray, placing all our hope in Him right now.

Heavenly Father, You made me to soar.
Life sometimes wants to keep me grounded,
but today I choose to rise up with my hope in You.
Your strength never fails . . . thank You!
Please help me lean on Your strength, not my own.
And help me communicate Your truth
to others, too.
I love You, Jesus. Amen.

Love Is Deliberate

I wanted those sheets there while I had my cup of tea,
one final reminder of the kindness of my father, of how,
during his last moments on earth, he was thinking of me
and how he could best welcome me home.

BOX OF BUTTERFLIES

My Father's house has many rooms; if that were not so,
would I have told you that I am going there
to prepare a place for you?
And if I go and prepare a place for you,
I will come back and take you to be with Me that you
also may be where I am.

JOHN 14:2–3

Random acts of kindness are brilliant; flooding the world with spontaneous displays of grace is a wonderful way to reveal God to a hurting world. *Deliberate acts of love* are another way to show people Who God is and what He does.

The evening before his death, my father and I spoke on the telephone. I was studying theater in London and had planned a trip home to see Dad and celebrate the ordination of my half brother John. On our brief call, my father—a man of few words at the best of times—said how glad he was that I was coming home and that, because of the ever-present dampness in our Derry air, he had hung my favorite yellow flannel sheets to air them out. In Ireland, we were rarely able to dry anything outside due to the rainy weather, so people in our town had indoor clotheslines, usually in the kitchen where there might be a stove to provide warmth and dryness. Preparing for my homecoming, Dad had placed my favorite sheets on our indoor line.

I went to bed that night imagining the soft, cozy feel of those flannel sheets, prepared for me by my loving father, but I was awakened in the middle of the night by a phone call from my brother, Lawrence. He told me that our dad's heart had given out suddenly; I would be coming home to bury my da, not celebrate with him.

I flew home to Ireland on the same flight but with a different purpose and a heavy heart. I entered our home and slipped into our kitchen to steel myself with the courage that only a cup of tea can give, when a vision took my breath away. There, hanging on the clothesline to air, were my favorite yellow flannel sheets. I held them to my face, breathed in their kindness, and cried. My earthly father thoughtfully prepared for my return. He never had the chance to see me come home, but his deliberate act of kindness reached me nonetheless.[39]

In John 14, Jesus promises that our Heavenly Father is preparing for us. In perfect loving-kindness, He is making ready for our return. And when we arrive, He will be there to welcome us home forever. Perhaps the kettle will be singing, the tea steeping, and our favorite sheets hanging to air.

Heavenly Father, I'm so grateful for Your
loving-kindness.
Thank You for preparing a place for us.
Thank You that where You are we will be also.
Thank You for the promises of forever safety,
forever love, forever peace.
Please help me to deliberately show love
and kindness to others.
May Your love help others always feel
at home with me.
In Jesus' name, amen.

Love Makes Us Whole

*When my mother died, I missed her so much that there
was truly a hole in me; the woman I became just grew
up around that "hole." But it was as if Reilly's birth put a
"w" in front of that word and made me "whole" again.*

BOX OF BUTTERFLIES

*See what great love the Father has lavished on us, that we
should be called children of God! And that is what we are!*

1 JOHN 3:1

I heard: "It's a girl," and tears streamed down my face. As I stared
down at my sweet baby, something happened within me. I held
a miracle in my arms! And still there was more: something I so
desperately missed was now restored. I cried in that moment for the
mother I had lost and the mother I had now become. I named her
Reilly, to honor my mother, Maureen O'Reilly.[40]

There is no question that love is a healer. It began with Reilly's
birth; and in the years since, love has filled and touched all the old
hurts within me. Through Reilly, God brought me healing.

Motherhood opened a deep well of love in me, love I didn't know
I had access to. Becoming a mother also helped my faith grow and
deepen because it has given me insight into how much God loves
us. I finally understood just how perfectly and unconditionally God

loves each and every one of us. We are, after all, His special children. The depth of my love for Reilly amazes me. And, of course, I then marvel at God's love for us.[41]

First John 3:1 describes God's love being "lavished" on us. The dictionary defines the verb "lavish" in this way: "to give in great amounts or without limits." God's love never holds back. It never stops giving. It's a love without limits. How glorious to be loved in this way! And by the God Who created the oceans and galaxies? Dear one, it takes my breath away.

You are loved with a lavish love by a perfect Father. You are His beloved child. Whatever your history, however you grew up and live now, lavish and healing love is available to you right now.

Jesus died for your sins *because of love*. The Holy Spirit is with you each and every day *because of love*. The Father's arms always stretch wide to receive you *because of love*. His love heals and makes whole.

Will you live like you are loved today?

Thank You, Heavenly Father,
for loving us unconditionally and perfectly.
We bring every unhealed hurt to You right now.
Please heal us with Your lavish love.
We are so grateful to be Your beloved children.
We open our hearts to receive more of Your love today.
Help us love others in ways that heal them.
In Jesus' name, amen.

Love Is Real

"This is my *mommy, not TV mommy."*

BOX OF BUTTERFLIES

A new command I give you: Love one another. As I have loved you, so you must love one another. By this everyone will know that you are My disciples, if you love one another.

JOHN 13:34–35

Once, while I was shopping in a local mall, someone asked me for an autograph. My daughter, Reilly, who was only four at the time, tugged at my hand and said, "This is *my* mommy, not TV mommy."

Every child, every person, needs to know that they are special, that they matter, that they are valued. Reilly expressed, at four years old, what we all long for—real and abiding love, not a show or an act.

We need someone Who weeps with us when our hearts are breaking, Who comforts us when storms rage. We long for someone Who can give us strength when we're weak, Who will keep us anchored when we're in danger of drifting.

Ultimately, we all need and want God. Only He can love perfectly.

He also asks us to love others as He has loved us. And this means loving people in a way that communicates they really matter, they are important, they are worth spending time and energy to love. By this, Jesus tells us in John 13:34–35, the whole world will know that we follow Him.

How I love others matters, not just for my life, but for the life of the world. Pretty radical, isn't it?

In that tender moment at the mall with my daughter, Reilly needed assurance that she belonged to me and I to her. My love could give her that confidence. Who in your life might need to feel that love and assurance from you? Is it a child? A friend? Your spouse or another family member?

God places people in our lives and calls us to love them. Sometimes it's easy to love; other times it's a significant challenge. But God never commands us to do something that He doesn't also empower us to do. Because He's commanded us to love as He has loved, we can trust that He'll give us the ability and the wisdom to love others in a way that communicates how important and special they are.

Today, and every day, let's commit to loving like Jesus loves us.

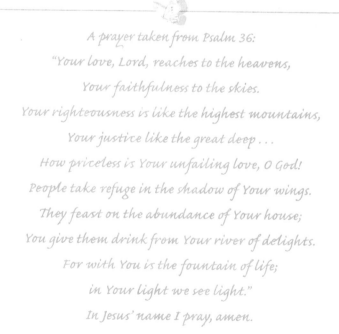

A prayer taken from Psalm 36:
"Your love, Lord, reaches to the heavens,
Your faithfulness to the skies.
Your righteousness is like the highest mountains,
Your justice like the great deep . . .
How priceless is Your unfailing love, O God!
People take refuge in the shadow of Your wings.
They feast on the abundance of Your house;
You give them drink from Your river of delights.
For with You is the fountain of life;
in Your light we see light."
In Jesus' name I pray, amen.

Love Cancels Loneliness

Love makes a family, not DNA or background. Love.
Just love. Simply love.

BOX OF BUTTERFLIES

God sets the lonely in families . . .

PSALM 68:6A

Reilly grew up surrounded by love. Della doted on her as a grandmother. Our co-star, Johnny Dye, was the perfect "Uncle Johnnie." Reilly adored her nanny, Debbie, and my assistant, Linda. We even enjoyed family visits from Ireland or trips across the pond, where Reilly could meet her Irish relatives and learn about the country and culture that shaped me. And while Reilly's dad and her older half sister, Vanessa, did not live in our town, Reilly saw them and knew they loved her.

Amid all this love, Reilly and I were best buddies and incredibly close.

We had a beautiful life in almost every way, but we were often on our own.

I knew Reilly felt confused when she compared our family with the families of her friends at school. It certainly didn't help when another child told my daughter that we weren't a "real" family because there were just the two of us. Reilly cried telling me this story, and my mama heart broke.

I assured Reilly that it's *love* that defines a family. I shared with her that my family growing up didn't look "normal." My mommy died when I was only ten. Raised only by my daddy, I understood how she felt. This seemed to comfort my precious girl and she vowed, "It's me and you, Mama. We are a family."

Years later, after Mark and I brought our families together, I remembered this painfully sweet encounter with Reilly. I didn't know then that God would bless me with an amazing husband and two fine stepsons. I had no idea that God would spread His love so wide that we would eventually share a Thanksgiving meal with my ex-husband and his nephew as well as Mark's ex-wife and her father. To most people, this kind of love sounds impossible.

Nothing is impossible for God.

Psalm 68 promises that our loving Heavenly Father "sets the lonely in families." These families don't always share blood. They share a deeper bond—Love.

Today you may find yourself tremendously grateful for the family you have. You may be experiencing a great deal of heartache because you are alone. If you are lonely today, reach out in prayer; ask Him to fulfill His promise to put you in a loving family. If you know someone lonely, perhaps God is asking you to draw that person in, giving them the chance to be loved like family. Wherever you're at, I invite you to open your heart to the love God would like to lavish on you and pour through you.

Precious Father, thank You for the gift of love.
Your Son, Jesus, made us part of Your family
with the bond of love.
I'm so grateful that Your love makes families
in so many unique ways.
Thank You that no one must stay lonely;
we can always reach out to and trust in You.
Help us to do that today. In Your name, amen.

Love Starts Small

The most magical things can have the humblest of beginnings. The magic of my love story with Mark began with my feet in a bucket of water. Not the most glamorous of images, I know, but a girl needs a pedicure every now and then!

BOX OF BUTTERFLIES

*Do not despise these small beginnings,
for the Lord rejoices to see the work begin.*

ZECHARIAH 4:10, NLT

If given the opportunity to plan how I'd meet the love of my life, I wouldn't have chosen to wear a tracksuit . . . with an elastic waistband of all things. But there I was, with my feet soaking wet and my cheeks flushed from catching eyes with the handsome man having his hair cut across the salon. His joy was contagious. This was a man *fully alive.*

Pause for a moment and travel way back to the second century, when a man of God named Irenaeus wrote: *"Gloria enim Dei vivens homo."*[42] Because I don't speak Latin, and I'm guessing you don't, either, let me give you an interpretive translation for that: "The glory of God is a man fully alive." Though I didn't know it at the time, I was attracted to Mark, my beloved husband, because he was full of life and enthusiasm. The word "enthusiasm" has its roots in a Greek term that means "to be full of God." Isn't that wonderful?

What would it look like for you to be fully alive, to be full of God? To be so alive that others are drawn to your winsome love and joy?

Before you feel overwhelmed by how to make that happen, think about starting small. This is how God often moves. In the smallest of beginnings, Jesus came to earth as a baby, yet He grew up to love and die for us.

When you think about it, love usually starts with small beginnings. A girl getting a pedicure encounters a man fully alive in God. A newborn is placed in his mother's arms, and love fills her to overflowing. A little chat over coffee at church eventually grows into lifelong friendship. Zechariah 4:10 tells us not to despise small beginnings. And I believe becoming a person *fully alive* in Jesus' love starts small.

Spend a few quiet moments with God right now. Ask Him to show you how to "start small" to love more.

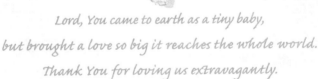

Lord, You came to earth as a tiny baby,
but brought a love so big it reaches the whole world.
Thank You for loving us extravagantly.
You love us so much that You died for us.
We are eternally grateful.
Thank You for helping us love others.
We can do nothing without You.
Please show me a small step of love to take today.
I want to be fully alive for Your glory.
In Jesus' name, amen.

Love Knows

Despite the fact that we hadn't shared the news of our wedding with our friends, planning instead to send a marriage announcement after the fact, a gift arrived.

BOX OF BUTTERFLIES

You have searched me, Lord, and You know me.
You know when I sit and when I rise, You perceive my thoughts from afar.
You discern my going out and my lying down; You are familiar with all my ways.

PSALM 139:1–3

Mark and I got married in our own backyard, with only our most intimate family in attendance. My daughter, Reilly, was bridesmaid and Mark's sons, James and Cameron, were best man and ring bearer. Della, who presided over the ceremony, was there with her husband, Franklin, and Mark's dad, Archie, was there with his wife, Jean, Mark's much-loved stepmom. Just a small and loving group. We said our vows under a beautiful arbor in our backyard, into which I had sewn three silk butterflies to represent my parents and Mark's mom, all of whom had passed away.

Earlier that morning, as Mark and I gazed out at the ocean saying prayers of gratitude for our special day, three beautiful butterflies had flown right in front of us. We were sure they were a sign of God's presence and our loved ones' spirits. Then, when Della arrived, she carried with her a lovely ornate purse with butterflies embroidered all over it. Later in the day a gift arrived—a picture frame with three butterflies in the corner.

On the *Touched by an Angel* set, we used to quote words attributed to Einstein: "Coincidence is God's way of remaining anonymous." I don't think my wedding day blessings were coincidental. On this day I felt so known, so seen, so loved by God.

There's nothing quite like a love that *knows*. When we feel known by someone—the way I felt known in such an intimate way through all that God brought together on my wedding day—there's simply nothing that compares.

The Bible tells us that God knows each of us. In fact, He knows every single hair on our heads! He knows our every action and every thought. He is familiar with all our ways. For some people, that can seem rather intimidating, but it doesn't have to be. God looks on us with perfect knowledge *and* perfect love. He does not look to find fault or to scold but rather to uphold us with love and compassion, truth and grace.

Because this is how God loves us, we are called to love others in the same way. As He has loved us, let us love one another. God has placed people around you—people He's called you to *know* and *love*. Dear one, who is it time for you to know and love better? Would you be willing to ask God to show you? Let's pray for His help right now.

Heavenly Father,
thank You for knowing everything about us.
Thank You for loving us.
You are so merciful, kind, and good.
Please help me to know and love You.
Help me to show Your love to others
by knowing them.
In Jesus' name, amen.

Love Looks Out

Love does not consist in gazing at each other but in looking outward together in the same direction.

ANTOINE DE SAINT-EXUPÉRY[33]

Two are better than one, because they have a good return for their labor.

ECCLESIASTES 4:9

If you attend enough weddings, you may hear these words read in the service or used in the toast. Both Ecclesiastes' and Saint-Exupéry's words beautifully express the truth that God did not intend for us to live on our own. We are a people designed for collaboration, for togetherness. We were made to give and receive *love* because God Himself *is love*.

You may not know that Antoine de Saint-Exupéry actually wrote the sentiment above, often attributed only to romance or marriage, about a love far more inclusive—the love of shared labor and sacrifice, love committed to a goal higher than oneself. The full quote reads: "No man can draw a free breath who does not share with other men a common and disinterested ideal. Life has taught us that Love does not consist in gazing at each other but in looking outward together in the same direction. There is no comradeship except through union in the same high effort. Even in our age of material well-being this must be so . . ."

God made us to share life, to share love. We are called by our Heavenly Father to unite with others "in the same high effort." In our digital and information age, when discord and distrust are so prevalent, we desperately need to unite under the "common and disinterested ideal" of loving others as we have been loved by God.

It brings me great joy to love Mark as his wife. Our romantic love is only one aspect of the love God asks us to bring into the world, though. I thank God that I love working alongside my husband to bring light through our work. That's why we named our production company LightWorkers Media. Jesus is the Light of the World, and we are His workers. You are His worker, too.

Who has God placed in your life? With whom might Jesus be inviting you to work toward something higher and greater than you could do on your own? Whether you're married or single, part of a huge family or an only child, God has set you in a specific sphere of influence. He made you to join with the people around you to bring His light and love to this world.

True, it's a lot easier to look no further than the person we're having coffee with, but God invites us to a far greater adventure. Will you follow His call to turn outward and work with others for His glory and good?

Heavenly Father, thank You for giving us
the capacity to give and receive love.
Thank You for inviting us to share in Your work
and equipping us to do what You've called us to do.
Please help me work with others to bring more light and
love into this world.
In Jesus' name, amen.

Love Never Fails

Who you are is perfect. God made you that way. He loves who you are becoming on the inside. The body will fade away. That's what it was made to do. Your heart and spirit will be with you forever.

BOX OF BUTTERFLIES

Love never fails. But where there are prophecies, they will cease; where there are tongues, they will be stilled; where there is knowledge, it will pass away . . . And now these three remain: faith, hope and love. But the greatest of these is love.

1 CORINTHIANS 13:8 AND 13

Despite our best efforts or how much we rail against the truth, every material substance fades. Things break down; our bodies decay; nothing lasts forever on this crazy and beautiful planet. Still, humans spend a great deal of time trying to maintain things. We paint our houses, replace our cars, buy new clothes with the hope that wearing something new will make us feel new. We purchase creams for our faces and workout gear aplenty. Nothing is inherently wrong with this. We do, after all, live in a physical world.

But in the end, only spiritual things *endure*. Only faith, hope, and love *never fail*. One day your earthly body will be no more, but the heart and spirit God placed in you will last *forever*. God loves who He made you to be. He wants to spend all of eternity with you. Isn't that wonderful?

Since this is true, don't you think we should spend more time attending to our hearts and our spirits than anything else? It only makes sense considering these are our eternal gifts. And yet, so often, we neglect these essential aspects of our being. We get on with the busyness of everyday life and forget that cultivating a heart and spirit of love takes time and effort.

Consider Mother Teresa, a woman who aged gracefully. Her beauty was apparent until the day she died. It glowed in the warmth of her smile as she helped God's people. She was radiant. She emitted a light that you cannot buy in a bottle. She displayed the true beauty of grace, compassion, and love.[44]

Do you think Mother Teresa became this way by accident? Of course not! She cultivated the beauty of love day after day. I don't know about you, but I would much rather follow her example than chase after the fading things of this world. What about you, dear one?

Lord God,

thank You for faith, hope, and love.

Your love never fails.

Things fall apart here on earth,

but You have given us eternal life.

Thank You for making my heart and my spirit.

Help me to cultivate a life of love,

for Your glory.

In Jesus' name, amen.

Love Never Dies

*They that love beyond the world cannot
be separated by it. Death cannot kill
what never dies.*

WILLIAM PENN, *MORE FRUITS OF SOLITUDE*

*Therefore what God has joined together,
let no one separate.*

MARK 10:9

Afton accompanying Della home from the hospital, I helped fill her rooms with flowers, gospel music, and prayer. But I wanted to do one more thing, something I knew would mean the world to Della. I wanted to bring her husband, Franklin, home from the hospital so that they could say a final good-bye.

I spoke with the clinicians caring for Franklin and discussed how to make this happen. Honestly, I would have been willing to "break him out," but I was relieved that wouldn't be necessary. I received permission to pick Franklin up, provided that I return him to his caretakers a few hours later.

George, a member of our staff, drove me in a large SUV to Franklin's care facility and pulled into the area where I'd been told to wait. A kind nurse wheeled Franklin outside, but her smile faltered when she saw our vehicle.

"I'm so sorry, but you aren't allowed to transport Franklin in anything but a wheelchair-accessible car."

My stomach immediately knotted. I did not want to let Della down, so I was unwilling to accept defeat. This was far too important.

I called my husband's office, my office, and some girlfriends, immediately employing additional brainpower to solve this problem. I also called on some faith warriors, asking them—truly begging them—to pray for a miracle. Franklin, sitting in his wheelchair, began to shift uncomfortably.

"Lord, please help," I prayed.

Within moments, a handicapped-accessible minivan taxi rambled down the street, and I launched myself into the middle of the road.

I quickly spoke with the driver, who was en route to pick up another resident. Fishing in my wallet, I pulled out some cash and pressed it into his hand, begging him to please come back. Fifteen minutes later, he did.

When we arrived at the Reese-Lett home, I picked a beautiful flower from their garden and placed it in Della's hair. She and Franklin spent quiet time together while I waited outside, praying with other friends who loved Della and had gathered at their house.

God brought Della and Franklin together. Their love came from God Himself. That could never be stolen by death. Their final earthly good-bye might better be called the first step toward an eternity of hellos.

Love is a miracle, dear one. There's no other way to understand it. And love brings miracles. There was no reason for a taxi to be on the street near Franklin's care facility. Even a flower to place in a beloved one's hair is a miracle of love if only we have eyes to see it.

Will you stop with me and thank God for the miracle of love that transcends death?

Beloved Jesus, You died so that we can
live eternally.
Thank You so much.
Thank You that Your love never fails.
Thank You that love does not end with death.
I am so grateful that You are love.
Please help me to see the miracles
around me today.
Amen.

Love Is a Verb

*I know without a doubt that love is a verb. Anyone can
say the words "I love you," but love is an action.*

BOX OF BUTTERFLIES

*Dear children, let us not love with words or speech but
with actions and in truth.*

1 JOHN 3:18

When our children were young, Mark and I took the whole family to Australia. We wandered the streets of Sydney, humming with unfamiliar sights and sounds. It was magical.

I can't recall who spotted it first, but within a few moments all five of us had gathered in front of a shop window. Displayed behind the glass was a painting that took our breath away. It was of a dog, but not just any dog. The painter had captured an Irish wolfhound so closely resembling our dog, Finn, that he could have been staring right back at us. Surrounding him were three perfectly painted butterflies.

Instantly I hatched a plan.

After we got back to the hotel, while the kids lounged off their jet lag, Mark stepped into an adjoining room to make business calls. I slipped out, made my way to the shop, and purchased the painting, planning to give it to Mark for his upcoming birthday. Sneaking back into our suite, I quickly showed the kids, swore them to secrecy, and stowed the painting.

When Mark's birthday arrived and he opened the present, the first words out of his mouth were "I can't believe it." Laughing with joy, he told me how he'd returned to the shop to buy the painting for me. He knew how much butterflies mean to me, and this painting had three—one to symbolize each of our children. The only problem? The painting had already been purchased . . . by me!

Mark and I look back on this story and marvel at the blessings of love—God's love for us and the love He's given us for one another. I'm so grateful to be married to Mark; he shows love actively. We had the same loving instinct and followed that tug from God to love one another.

Sometimes a loving impulse crosses our mind and we put it off, only to forget it altogether. Other times we doubt whether our love will be meaningful to someone. I've learned, however, that love takes action. My father always said that love is a verb, and I've lived my life by the truth he taught me.

I believe there's someone God will place on your mind after reading this story. I believe He'll tug at your heart, inviting you to show that person love. How will you respond?

Heavenly Father, it's amazing to be loved by You!

Thank You for loving us every single day.

You show Your love and ask us to show Your love to others.

I want to love, not just with words but with my actions.

Whom would you like me to love today?

Help me to love everyone, including myself, in Your name.

Amen.

Love Surrenders All

*To love at all is to be vulnerable. Love anything and
your heart will be wrung and possibly broken.*

C. S. LEWIS, *THE FOUR LOVES*

*Then Simeon blessed them, and he said to Mary, the
baby's mother, "This child . . . has been sent as a sign
from God, but many will oppose him. As a result, the
deepest thoughts of many hearts will be revealed.
And a sword will pierce your very soul."*

LUKE 2:35, NLT

As Mark and I prepared to bring the Bible to television, we
spent weeks searching for the right actress to portray Jesus'
mother, Mary. As I scrolled and sifted through headshots
and resumés, Mark shocked me with the simple observation, "I don't
know why you are missing the obvious. You need to take on this role
yourself."

I had never even considered this. I was serving as producer on *The
Bible* project, not as an actress. I also knew it would be an incredible
honor and privilege, not to mention a huge challenge, to portray Mary.
Despite initial surprise at the idea, my heart leapt at the invitation God
extended as I prayed and asked for His clarity. Apparently, He wanted
me to take on the role, but not know about it ahead of time.

Entering Mary's world in such an intimate way, studying her life, and embodying it day after day transformed me. I learned so many things from Jesus' mother. Perhaps what I learned most intently was that love is vulnerable, that love sacrifices.

When Jesus was dedicated at the Temple in Jerusalem, the prophet Simeon told Mary that "a sword will pierce your very soul." Simeon spoke, three decades prior, of Jesus' death on the Cross for us.

It must have been unbearable for Mary to see her own son being crucified. Yet she showed such faith and courage. Imagine the faith she must have possessed to not completely fall apart at the foot of the Cross. There, up there, was her baby boy! There was the son she had raised and nurtured and loved so much. While Jesus paid the ultimate sacrifice, sweet, tender Mary also made a sacrifice.[45]

After hearing Simeon's words, Mary could have lived in constant fear, waiting for the sword that would pierce her soul. But when we look at her life in the Bible, we know that Mary chose love instead.

Love dares to sacrifice. Love dares to trust, even when death seems like it's won the day. I believe God is inviting us, today, to stop and trust Him with the sacrifice Love asks us to make.

Dear Jesus, love is so beautiful;

it can also be so painful.

I don't want to close my heart off to love,

even if it means sacrifice.

Thank You for the example of Your beautiful mother, Mary.

Like Mary, please help me to trust You and to love

even when it's hard.

In Your name I pray, amen.

Love Sets You Free

*Don't ever underestimate the power of forgiveness.
I've seen it free people. I've seen it lift burdens that had
weighed them down and kept them from moving on.*

BUFFY ANDREWS, *A GRANDMOTHER'S LEGACY*

*Since God cares for you, let Him carry all
your burdens and worries.*

1 PETER 5:7, VOICE

Many years ago, I was burdened by a heavy weight.

Someone had hurt me . . . as deeply as I could imagine being hurt . . . and I didn't know how the wound would ever heal. I had begun to believe that the tear in my heart would never mend, that I would be like an amputee who must compensate for a missing limb; I would simply learn to live with it.

Only problem was, that wasn't working.

The weight of pain on my soul didn't just injure me. It affected my ability to love others the way I wanted to. As a follower of Christ, I knew the only way forward was forgiveness.

But our world is full of misunderstandings about forgiveness. We sometimes believe that forgiveness means what happened to us was okay. It's not! We often feel that, if we let go of our pain, we'll lose power over the one who hurt us. The reverse is true! The one who injured still controls us if we don't embrace God's forgiveness, which sets us free.

I suppose that's what is at the heart of the matter: forgiveness isn't as much for the "other person"; forgiveness is first and most for me.

As this truth began to work its way into my mind and heart, I set the burden down. I could only lay it down for brief stretches at first. But, as time went on, I discovered that the burden had become lighter. Eventually, one day I can't even clearly remember, I learned that I did not need to pick the burden up . . . ever again.

Beloved one, I know that you may have experienced trauma, anger, or pain because of someone else's choices. I weep for you who have suffered. Let's not allow an inability to forgive to keep us hostage to the burden of pain and unhappiness that we are carrying. I know it can feel frightening to lay the burden of bitterness down; perhaps you've carried it as long as you can remember. It's time to trust God and let Him carry the weight. It's time, dear friend.

I love *The Voice*'s translation of 1 Peter 5:7, which uses such vivid imagery to communicate, "Since God cares for you, let Him carry all your burdens and worries." There's no question *if* God cares for you. The matter is settled. *Since* He cares for you, you can trust Him to carry *all* your burdens and worries. Let's pray about this now.

Thank You, precious Lord,

for inviting us to lay our burdens down.

Thank You for caring about us.

Thank You for promising to bear every weight and worry.

You are so kind, so loving.

Please remove any burden of unforgiveness from my heart.

Please set me free.

In Jesus' name I pray. Amen.

Love Is Unconditional

The dog is the most faithful of animals and would be much esteemed were it not so common. Our Lord God has made his greatest gift the commonest.

FROM MARTIN LUTHER'S *TABLE TALK*

Every good and perfect gift is from above, coming down from the Father of the heavenly lights, Who does not change like shifting shadows.

JAMES 1:17

When I pray, I am never alone. Jesus is with me, yes. I also have three precious dogs who join me on almost every occasion: Red and Max, our English Labs, and Ruby, our giant Irish wolfhound. My lovely dog family must have quite the devotional life, as they lie at my feet morning after morning, soaking in love as I spend time in the presence of God.

Like many of you, I consider my pets a great gift from God. Dogs may be common in the sense that they surround us—in homes across the world—but, as Luther observed, God often makes his greatest gifts the commonest. I love my dogs' unique personalities, the way they make me laugh and the way they make me feel.

How many lessons I've learned from my dogs . . . I could scarcely count them. Chief among them: unconditional love. Red, Max, and Ruby may watch me leave with a befuddled sadness—*Why would she go* anywhere? they seem to wonder (particularly after the COVID-19 lockdown, when they had me all day, every day!)—but when I return, nothing but love greets me. Dogs love without bitterness or any real expectations. They don't shame us or guilt us. They give love and desire to receive it. What a beautiful picture they paint of unconditional love.

James 1:17 tells us that every good gift comes down from our Heavenly Father. God graciously gives us dogs and dancing, cats and clouds and cookies, common yet precious things. He also gives an unconditional love that never alters course. As James puts it, God "does not change like shifting shadows."

When my dogs welcome me home, wagging their tails excitedly, it reminds me of Luke 15, when Jesus describes the perfect father, who enthusiastically welcomes home both the son who has wandered and that son who has not. God's love does not change based on what we've done. His love does not shift like shadows.

Jesus also calls us to love one another as He loves us. That sometimes feels daunting. I wonder if we could take one step forward by loving others like our dogs love us. Theirs is a simple love, unencumbered by the heavy weight of expectations or long memory. How different might our world be if we chose to love a little more like this. Will you please pray with me about it?

Lord, thank You for every good and perfect gift.
Thank You for the gifts of pets!
We are so thankful for the love they show us.
And we're so thankful—so incredibly thankful—for Your
unconditional love.
You never change like a shifting shadow.
We love You and we can trust You.
In Jesus' name. Amen.

Love Lets Go

*When we let go and empty our hands, God is there to fill
our open hands.*

BOX OF BUTTERFLIES

*There is a time for everything,
and a season for every activity under the heavens:
a time to be born and a time to die,
a time to plant and a time to uproot . . .
a time to tear down and a time to build.*

ECCLESIASTES 3:1–3

I decided to move back to California after *Touched by an Angel* wrapped. I had been filming the series in Utah for over nine years and I felt uncertain about what my next steps should be. It was a prayerful time of soul-searching and trusting God for guidance. The winds of change were blowing, allowing me an opportunity to discover a deeper sense of self, free now of the attention that had rained down on me for many years because of the success of the show. While we were filming the series, I had tried to stay grounded in gratitude, but the truth is, once the filming stopped, life seemed very quiet indeed.

God spoke so tenderly to me during this season. He reminded me that I am not what I do or how I look, that my worth was not attached to the role I had played. He reminded me that I am His beloved child. Without His love, I don't believe I could have let go.

Ecclesiastes 3 tells us that "there is a time for everything / . . . a time to plant and a time to uproot . . . / a time to tear down and a time to build." Most of us prefer the "planting" and "building" seasons. We're slow to sign up for the tearing down and uprooting; we're definitely leery of the "time to die" bit. All of this, however, is part of God's glorious plan of love.

In order to know and experience more of God's love, we must learn to embrace seasons of letting go. It's difficult, I know. But God is in *every* season of my life, whether it's nine seasons of TV success or the years that immediately followed, being carpool queen for my daughter and stepsons. He is with us in every season.

Please take a moment and close one of your hands. Make a tight fist.

If we live like this, if we grasp our life tightly, we may feel slightly more in control. But how much can get into a closed fist? Almost nothing! Only living with open hands and open hearts allows us to receive God's love.

Living openly may feel unnerving, but it's also incredibly freeing. Today, trusting God's love, I invite you to open your hand and open your heart. If you've lived tightly for many years, God will treat you kindly, helping you to open a little more each day. I lovingly encourage you to not resist Him, no matter what season you are in. Let go and open your hands and your heart to His healing love.

Father in heaven,
I'm so grateful that You are completely
trustworthy.
Please help me to open my hands and my
heart completely to You.
Take away any fear I have about holding on.
Your love gives me confidence and peace.
Your love reassures me and strengthens me.
Whatever the future may hold I will
not be afraid,
because I know You are with me.
Thank You for always guiding me and
lighting the path.
Amen.

Stillness

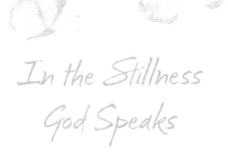

In the Stillness God Speaks

God's image is reflected in nature all around us, and when we are quiet, when we connect to the stillness within ourselves, we can hear Him speak.

BOX OF BUTTERFLIES

Be still, and know that I am God.

PSALM 46:10

Every day, God is speaking.

Through the delightful beauty of the butterfly, God is speaking. Through the silver majesty of a harvest moon, God is speaking. Through the crashing waves of the ocean, through the smile of a beloved friend, through His Word of life and hope, God is speaking.

Can you hear Him, dear one?

Do you believe that He speaks messages of love, comfort, and hope to you?

I know that He does.

He wants you to hear—every single day—that you are treasured, honored, and beloved (Isaiah 43:4). Whether you're currently experiencing high times or hard ones, He wants you to hear His voice and know that *you are* never *alone*. The Bible promises this. "The Lord Himself goes before you and will be with you; He will never leave you nor forsake you. Do not be afraid; do not be discouraged" (Deuteronomy 31:8).

God is speaking, but we sometimes find it difficult to hear His voice, don't we?

The truth is, we are sometimes too busy to hear God speak. Other times, pain or shame drowns out His voice. Regardless of where we're at in our lives, God continues to speak words of love, peace, and truth. I have learned that, to hear Him, I must deliberately let go of the noise all around me.

When life begins to get messy and chaotic and loud, I have to take time away. I have to find a moment of stillness. And I find that stillness through prayer and in nature, where I can be quiet and listen. I wholeheartedly agree with the words attributed to T. S. Eliot: "If we really want to pray, we must first learn to listen, for in the silence of our hearts God speaks."[46]

Take a deep, cleansing breath with me today. For this moment, find a place of stillness. Let go of all that separates you from God's love. Listen for His voice.

You are treasured . . . you are loved . . . you are never *alone.*

I invite you today to deliberately let go of the noise around you. Even if it's only for a sliver of time, get away and meet with God in the beauty of His creation. Take a walk and look at the flowers or listen for birds singing. If you're not able to be outside, open a window and feel the breeze on your face. God is speaking to you, dear one. Why not take a moment to listen?

Thank You, Father, for Your marvelous creativity.
This world is bursting with beauty.
We're so grateful for all the blessings You've
given us in nature.
Thank You for speaking to us with a voice of
tender love and care.
Please allow us to hear You today,
and to know that we are cherished, honored,
and loved . . .
always.
In Jesus' name, amen.

Stillness in Our Solitude

Prayer and solitude are ways to listen to the voice that speaks to our heart, in the center of our being . . . if you enter deeper and deeper into that place, you not only meet God, but you meet the whole world there.

HENRI NOUWEN, YOU ARE THE BELOVED[47]

Very early in the morning, while it was still dark, Jesus got up, left the house and went off to a solitary place, where He prayed.

MARK 1:35

When you read the word "solitude," what comes to mind? For many people, "solitude" has become synonymous with "loneliness." This is understandable, considering how disconnected and alienated many people feel in our loud, frenetic world.

For those who know and follow God, however, "solitude" can become synonymous with "thriving." Solitude and prayer are entry points through which God accesses the heart. God speaks to us there, in the most intimate and tender way.

Being alone in prayer isn't a lonely place; it's a place of stillness that enables us to hear God's voice. He calls us His beloved. He calls us precious. He calls us honored. And, oh, how we all need to hear that!

Our world is noisy and full of distractions. Sometimes—perhaps *often*—we must draw away, as Jesus did. True, it's not realistic for us to spend all our time in stillness and prayer. We cannot hear God's voice clearly, however, when we spend *zero* time in solitude and prayer.

When we're alone with God, it's easy to talk or ask. There are so many concerns on our hearts. There are an infinite number of needs in this hurting world. But being still before God also involves listening. And listening to God leads to life. The life-giving truths that we are loved without limit, that we are loved no matter what, that we are loved until the very end, empower us for the next adventure.

In Matthew 3:17, God the Father proclaims of Jesus, "This is My dearly loved Son, Who brings Me great joy" (NLT). Because God has adopted you as His child, these words are for you, too. You are His dearly loved child and you bring Him great joy.

Take a moment right now and draw in a deep, cleansing breath. Receive God's great love for you. Next, look at your calendar and plan a time when you can be alone with God. Take a notebook and write down what He tells you. Let His loving voice draw you deeper into the stillness. You'll find, as Henri Nouwen acknowledged, that not only is God there, but love for the whole world is there, too.

Thank You, Lord, for loving the whole world.
Each of us is Your beloved child.
Thank You for loving me so much that You
want to be with me.
Please help me to find a still point to
be with You.
Help me to hear Your voice, Holy Spirit.
May I live out of my identity as
Your beloved one
and help others do the same.
In Jesus' name, amen.

Stillness in the Storm

When darkness veils His lovely face,
I rest on His unchanging grace;
In every high and stormy gale,
My anchor holds within the veil.

EDWARD MOTE, "ON CHRIST THE SOLID ROCK I STAND," 1834

. . . by two unchangeable things in which it is
impossible for God to lie, we who have fled to take hold
of the hope set before us may be greatly encouraged.
We have this hope as an anchor for the soul.

HEBREWS 6:18–19

Mark and I founded our production company, LightWorkers Media, to tell stories of hope. Our goal is to create engaging, uplifting, and inspirational content that breaks through the clutter of modern life, building a community of sharing and igniting a movement in the real world that motivates people to celebrate and share the good all around them. We created LightWorkers because we've found peace and hope in God. Without hope, there is no future or, at the very least, not a future worth living. Though we've gone through some vicious storms in life, God keeps us anchored in His stillness—in peace and hope.

God Himself is the Hope of the World. And this hope, as Hebrews 6:19 describes it, is an anchor for our souls. Anchored in the hope, promises, and love of God, all of us can find safety from the storms of life. We can find a still point of internal peace, held fast by Jesus. Sometimes He stills the storm, but other times He stills us—His beloved children.

Mark and I live quite near the Pacific Ocean, and we regularly see boats anchoring offshore. With a sturdy anchor, no matter how large the ship, no matter how fierce the storm, it will stay put. To be secured appropriately, a boat must drop anchor deep below the surface, where tide and waves cannot sway it.

In a similar way, if we are not anchored spiritually in the timeless and changeless hope of God, we're in danger of drifting, possibly even crashing. God, Who Hebrews 6 reminds us *cannot* lie, promises that hope in Him anchors our soul.

Only in Him do we find the stillness of spirit that we need, despite the ebbing and flowing tide of our lives, despite the storms that may threaten us.

Dear friend, how anchored in God's hope would you say your life currently is? Your anchor will only hold if it's fastened deep below the surface of your life, in the precious soul God's given you. If you're not yet there, let's pray about it. And if you're already anchored securely, let's pray that you can help someone else find hope. That's what I try to do, and I pray you'll join me.

Oh, Lord, thank You for hope.

Your hope keeps us secure and gives us strength.

Thank You that we never have to face the storms of life alone.

Thank You for the promise of Your presence.

Please help me to stay anchored in Your hope.

Please help me to show others the power of hope in You.

Amen.

Stillness in Uncertainty

*Mark and I waited anxiously, holding each other close
and praying, as the doctor examined him. Cameron
was very brave, and though we tried to appear strong
in front of him, we were incredibly worried. After scans
and tests and hushed conversations, the doctor finally
pulled us aside to share his diagnosis.*

BOX OF BUTTERFLIES

*Wait for the Lord;
be strong and take heart
and wait for the Lord.*

PSALM 27:14

Sometimes you hear the words: "Everything's okay. The tests came back negative." You exhale and praise God and go back to life as you knew it.

For us, this was not that day.

That day, we received news no parents want to hear: "Your son has a brain tumor."

Cameron had taken a semester off college to work with us on the crew for *A.D. The Bible Continues*, a series Mark and I were producing together. We were thrilled to have him join us in Morocco and looked forward to sharing all the memories months of filming together would give us.

Instead, just a few weeks in, Cameron became very ill. We traveled to Malta, where we were simultaneously shooting another TV series, thinking the food or water in Morocco might have made him sick. Though Cameron improved for a short time, things quickly went from bad to worse.

After the doctors diagnosed Cameron's brain tumor, they counseled us to get him back to the States for surgery, so we arranged for a medical evacuation. When the plane touched down in Los Angeles, Cameron was taken directly to the hospital and the surgery was performed immediately.

His team of physicians and nurses worked tirelessly, but Mark and I could do virtually nothing. We had to wait and trust.

Sometimes, in the hustle and bustle of life, we long for stillness. Other times we wish for activity to distract us from something we can't control. Mark and I found ourselves in the latter of those two situations, wishing that we could *do* something, help in some way.

God was calling us to be still and trust Him to act.

The writer of Psalm 27, King David, urges us to wait for the Lord, to be strong and take heart. David himself learned to do this. In the same psalm David writes: "I remain confident of this: I will see the goodness of the Lord in the land of the living" (Psalm 27:13). Only when we cultivate confidence in God, trusting that He will act for our good and with our best in mind, can we wait and be still.

I'll not pretend that the waiting was easy. With trust in God, however, it was possible. Patiently trusting God is possible for you, too.

Thank You, Lord, for being perfectly trustworthy.
Your Word promises that I can wait
with confidence
because You will act with my best in mind.
It's difficult to trust sometimes, Lord, but
I want to rely on You more.
Please help me to be patient as I wait.
I need You, Lord.
In Jesus' name, amen.

Stillness in Surrender

Mark and I are both producers in our day-to-day lives;
members of the cast or crew come to us with situations
that need fixing, and we help to figure things out.

BOX OF BUTTERFLIES

. . . keep this command without spot or blame until the
appearing of our Lord Jesus Christ, which God will
bring about in His own time—
God, the blessed and only Ruler,
the King of kings and Lord of lords.

1 TIMOTHY 6:14-15

As producers, it's our job to solve problems, to make things happen, to move forward despite the obstacles. A producer controls a great deal of what happens on any given project. With Cameron's illness, though, Mark and I could control almost nothing, and we felt our lack of control . . . keenly.

Before this experience, I associated feeling out of control with complete chaos. In Cameron's illness, however, I also discovered a still point in the storm—a place where I was both powerless and still, invited by God to surrender my need for control.

If you're anything like me, losing control feels terrifying. How will you make it if you can't direct the traffic of your life, the course of your family's life? I learned that the only way to make it was by surrendering in the stillness. I needed to hand everything over to God. We were very grateful for an excellent medical team and extraordinary care for Cameron, but ultimately we had to hand over our fear and our confusion to God.

I love that, in 1 Timothy 6:14–15, God gives us the confidence we need to surrender control. Timothy promises that God will bring things about "in His own time." He also identifies God as "the *blessed* and *only* Ruler."

What does this mean?

Only God is in control.

And He is good at being in control. That's what the word "blessed" implies.

Have you ever noticed that when we're desperate for control, we aren't very good at keeping things together? We usually become anxious or irritable, bossing people around in our effort to fix/arrange/ solve whatever problem we're facing. We're not *blessed* controllers, are we? Only when we surrender the control we thought we had— which was, after all, an illusion, since God is the only one Who can control all things—do we find peace in the storms of life. Surrendering in the stillness calms the storm and calms us.

I'd love to pray this for us right now.

Lord, thank You for being the blessed and only
Ruler, the King of kings and Lord of lords.
We love You! We thank You!
You are so good at what You do.
When life spins out of control, please help us
surrender to You in the stillness.
Please help us remember to hand everything
over to You.
We can trust You, Lord. Thank You for that
truth and hope.
In Jesus' name. Amen.

Stillness in the Sanctuary

*We have always called our home "the Sanctuary," and if
ever we needed a space of peace and calm, it was now.*

BOX OF BUTTERFLIES

*I have seen You in the sanctuary and beheld Your power
and Your glory.*

PSALM 63:2

In the long, difficult days of Cameron's illness, Mark and I longed
for sanctuary, a safe place of refuge from the storm all around us.

Though our home had always been that place, during Cameron's hospitalization we faced some complicating factors. Before
we left to film in Morocco, we had started some renovation projects,
thinking it was the perfect time, as we would be out of the country
for several months. Now we were unexpectedly back, and our house
was in chaos. It was a shock to walk in and discover walls removed,
plastic sheeting all over the place, and a coating of dust everywhere.

We needed a sanctuary, but with builders in the house we certainly weren't going to find it at home. We thought about checking
into a hotel but ultimately decided we still wanted the comfort and
security that comes from being in our own home and being able to
crawl into our own bed. We would deal with the chaos, the physical
mess in our home that reflected so intensely what was going on in
our emotional and spiritual lives.[48]

Looking back, I see it as a mysterious but merciful working of God that we returned to a home that was far from a sanctuary. Because our home wasn't a place of stillness and refuge, we sought God even more. We needed more than external stillness in those agonizing days when Cameron lay in the hospital. We needed the kind of stillness that can only come in the arms of God, in the sanctuary of His presence.

Sometimes we can mask the chaos going on inside us. If everything looks good on the outside, we may be tempted to think, *I won't completely fall apart. If I can hold it together for another day, another week, another year,* then *maybe I can let go.*

Beloved one, we are never called to bear the burden of our own heartache. When there's a storm raging around or inside you, stillness with God is your safe place.

I realize that stillness can unnerve some of us. Facing our own thoughts, pain, or memories can be frightening. God understands. He calls you to seek Him and discover that, with Him, stillness inside enables you to face the tempest outside. Why not seek Him with me in prayer right now?

Jesus, we try to hold it together in so many ways,
but what we really need is You.
When we seek You in Your sanctuary, Your power
and glory fill us.
You enable us to face every storm with stillness
in our hearts.
Please guide us today to turn to You and nothing else.
You are everything we need.
In Your precious name we pray, amen.

Stillness Inside

*It was here, alone, where I could finally cry out to God
and try to find the stillness within myself.*

BOX OF BUTTERFLIES

*"Go out and stand before Me on the mountain," the
Lord told him. And as Elijah stood there, the Lord
passed by, and a mighty windstorm hit the mountain.
It was such a terrible blast that the rocks were torn
loose, but the Lord was not in the wind. After the wind
there was an earthquake, but the Lord was not in the
earthquake. And after the earthquake there was a fire,
but the Lord was not in the fire. And after the fire there
was the sound of a gentle whisper.*

1 KINGS 19:11–12, NLT

During the weeks leading up to and following Cameron's brain surgery, I remember driving back and forth from the hospital. Those times alone in the car provided my most intimate moments with God. There were times I had to pull over on the side of the road and sit in the quiet of my car, weeping and listening for His still, small voice. Only in the privacy of my car could my soul allow itself to feel.

I cried out to God in the stillness. *God, please heal Cameron. Please, Lord, please, please heal him.*

Reverend Billy Graham described prayer as a lifeline to God. This perfectly captures how I felt in those still, quiet moments in my car, crying out to God. Prayer connected me to God with a lifeline that I desperately needed.

When Cameron was in the hospital, our life felt like the scene described in 1 Kings 19, where God reveals Himself to the prophet Elijah. The mighty storm of Cameron's illness tore at and blasted us, but God was not in the wind. The foundations of our lives felt as if they were quaking, but God was not in the earthquake. He was not in the fire of fear. His voice was a gentle whisper, and I needed to be still to hear it.

All of us face times of severe testing. We feel the heat of the fire, the rocking of the earthquake, the icy blast of the cruel winds of suffering. God brings us through all this and reveals Himself with a still, small voice, the gentle whisper of His Spirit.

I understand how terribly difficult it can be to find stillness when the storm is raging. I found it in my car. Where can you find moments to be still and hear from the Lord, dear one? Listen for His gentle whisper. May the angry din of this world never silence His voice within you.

Almighty God, You are so powerful and holy,
yet You reveal Yourself in a gentle whisper,
with a still, small voice.
Holy Spirit, please attune our ears to Your grace and mercy.
May we hear the voice of Your love
above all the clatter of this world.
And may we speak to others the words of Your Spirit.
Amen.

Stillness in Solidarity

We could feel the love that surrounded us,
and we were uplifted and strengthened by it.

BOX OF BUTTERFLIES

For where two or three gather in My name,
there am I with them.

MATTHEW 18:20

Sometimes we need the stillness of solitude. Other times we need the stillness of solidarity. During Cameron's illness, God taught us about both.

I've already shared with you how times alone in the car became moments of worship as I cried out to God and allowed Him to still my anxious heart. Today I'd like to share with you how stillness in prayer with others can transform painful experiences.

After many long weeks, Mark, who stood watch over Cameron like a warrior angel morning, noon, and night, was just about worn out. All of us were exhausted. We were practically living at the hospital, and the uncertainty was frightening. Even while we relied on, trusted in, and sought God, our bodies weakened. Our spirits sometimes flagged.

Enter the people of God!

When our dear friends Pastor Rick and Kay Warren came by and prayed with us and over Cameron, it was not only a blessing to

Cameron, but it lifted our spirits as well. Indeed, we were so grateful to all the friends who rallied around us—those who visited and those who reached out to us on email or on the phone, and we were particularly grateful to all those who reached out to us in prayer.[49]

When we seek God with other believers, miraculous things happen. When we spend time in the stillness of God's presence with brothers and sisters in Christ, even if circumstances don't change, we are transformed.

The verse from Matthew reminds us that when we gather with even one other believer, Jesus meets us there. In the stillness of His presence, Christ moves in power. Mark and I will never forget the sense of being upheld in and covered by the prayers of God's people. The solidarity of those who loved us created a stillness that we could never have mustered on our own.

Never forget . . . you can be part of this for someone else!

Whom do you know who is sick or needy today? Why not reach out to a brother or sister in Christ who also knows that person? Pray together. Seek God's presence together and enjoy the stillness of solidarity. Jesus is with you. And He changes everything.

Jesus, thank You for the gift of prayer.
Thank You for the lifeline it gives us to You.
Thank You for how it connects us with others.
Thank You that we can find stillness with You
in solidarity
with those who pray with us and for us.
What a wonderful gift, Lord.
Please help us to give that gift to others.
In Your name, amen.

Stillness in the Waiting

Prayer is more than asking. It is a conversation with our Beloved.
It is a quieting of the soul, so we can hear.

BOX OF BUTTERFLIES

The Lord longs to be gracious to you; therefore He will rise up to show you compassion. For the Lord is a God of justice. Blessed are all who wait for Him!

ISAIAH 30:18

Prayer can mean so many things. It is most definitely the crying out to God for help, as I found myself doing in the car, desperately clinging to God's lifeline. In those dark days of uncertainty, all I could do was cry out, *Help Cameron, God. Please heal him, God.* I feel certain God welcomed those prayers. I believe He welcomes us anytime we come to Him, even if we have no words.

Indeed, when we have no words, our hearts may be more open to hear His voice, the still, small voice that Elijah heard long ago and that I heard as I wept in my car, the gentle whisper that I encouraged you to listen for, no matter what's going on or will go on in your life. I've learned that listening for God's voice in this way involves waiting for Him to speak and that takes time. We need to patiently wait for God to settle our hearts.

We are a nation of doers. Rather than human beings, we are human do-ings. We work and strive and talk and move and go, go, go. But if we want to be at peace, we must stop. We must wait for God. We need to wait in the stillness so that we can hear His voice.

We waited quite some time before we heard the wonderful words: "Cameron is doing well; we're discharging him from the hospital." I am overjoyed to share with you that, today, our son is whole and healed and doing great. We waited on God, and God brought us through the storm. He stilled our hearts as we waited, and we are forever grateful.

It's an incredible truth that God longs to bring all of us through the storms of life; He wants to show all of us compassion and justice. He desires to lovingly direct us; He is the best of Fathers, Who always gives his beloved children the right counsel at the right time. "Whether you turn to the right or to the left," God promises in Isaiah 30:21, "your ears will hear a voice behind you, saying, 'This is the way; walk in it.'"

If you look at the original Hebrew text for this passage, you'll discover that the same root word, *chakah*, "to wait," is used in both Isaiah 30:18 and 21.[50] Literally, God waits for us as we wait for Him. How beautiful! He yearns for you to come and listen. He awaits your arrival. He is eager to guide you. In the stillness, you will hear His voice. Why not take a moment to listen to Him right now?

Lord God, I quiet myself in Your presence now.

Thank You for waiting for me.

Thank You for longing to show me compassion.

Thank You for guiding me.

I need Your direction.

Please help me to breathe in and out right

now, taking time to listen to You.

I will wait for You.

In Jesus' name, amen.

Stillness in the Now

Stillness brings you into the present moment. We are often so fixated on something that happened in the past or worried about what might happen in the future that we completely miss the now.

BOX OF BUTTERFLIES

God said to Moses, "I AM WHO I AM. This is what you are to say to the Israelites: 'I AM has sent Me to you.'"

EXODUS 3:14

Prayer can involve a time that you set aside to commune with God. We need time to listen, to become still, and to wait on our loving Heavenly Father.

I also like to bring prayer into every moment, planned or unplanned. I want to call Him in, to invite Him into each moment. I feel this strongest when I'm in nature. When we are surrounded by beauty, we can commune with God and His creation. Walking in a field or looking up at the sky allows us to breathe and recharge; it reminds us how big our God is.

God is also in the small things . . . the song of a bird, the feel of the sun on our skin, the buzz of a bumblebee, the flight of a butterfly. In every blade of grass, we can see the beauty of creation. We find God in the now, in the present moment. We find God when we become still enough to be present in our own lives.

God reveals Himself as the ever-present and all-sufficient One in Exodus 3:14, when he commissions Moses. He asks Moses to take a message to Pharaoh, the most powerful ruler of that day, the sovereign who, with his fathers before him, had enslaved God's people for four hundred years.

Moses—quite understandably—felt intimidated by this job.

"Suppose I go to the Israelites," Moses pleads, "and say to them, 'The God of your fathers has sent me to you,' and they ask me, 'What is His name?' Then what shall I tell them?"

God replies, "Tell them I AM has sent Me to you."

God is the God of the past and the future. But He also *is*—presently—the Great I AM, God of the *now*.

When we invite God to reveal Himself in the moment, we discover a healing stillness like no other. God is with you right now. No matter where you are or what you're doing, He is present with you in all His perfection and power and love. So much love.

I invite you to pause and commune with God in the present moment. At some point today, get out and be with God in His beautiful creation. Let the ever-present I AM fill you with peace as you are still with Him.

Lord God, thank You for being present.

Thank You that there is nothing beyond You.

You are the God of now, the God of this very moment.

It's tough for me to stay present, Lord,

especially in times of difficulty.

Help me to be still—at peace—in Your arms of love.

I pray this in Jesus' name.

Amen.

Stillness in the Silence

*We rarely think of the air we breathe, yet it is in us
and around us all the time. In similar fashion, the
presence of God penetrates us, is all around us, is always
embracing us.*

THOMAS KEATING

*. . . the Holy Spirit prays for us with groanings that
cannot be expressed in words. And the Father who knows
all hearts knows what the Spirit is saying, for the Spirit pleads
for us believers in harmony with God's own will.*

ROMANS 8:26B–27, NLT

When I began writing *Box of Butterflies*, I reached out to my brother, Lawrence, to ask him about some memories. So many years had passed since our beloved mother went to be with Jesus; maybe things happened differently than I remembered? Lawrence certainly recalled, as clearly as I did, that we instinctively reached out to hold hands on the painful ride home after my mother's death.

"You've been reaching out to me across the ocean ever since," my brother said.

As we both experienced the same loss at such a young age, we had a deep connection, born out of a shared pain. Perhaps that's why his diagnosis with throat cancer hit me so very hard.

I booked a flight to Ireland and traveled to the hospital as quickly as I could. My brother wanted to be at home, on hospice care, but the doctors needed to stabilize him first.

Apart from the low hum of medical machinery and periodic beeps from various monitors, a deep quiet pervaded the room. Lawrence rested on the bed, and I entered silently, noticing the lovely green hills rolling outside the window. Ireland is a beautiful country, and I thanked God for this beautiful view. Fiona, Lawrence's wife, and my grown nieces, Laura and Lisa, kindly left to give us time alone together.

Because the cancer attacked Lawrence's throat, speaking had become quite difficult for him. He scratched out a few words, but it was clear that he was weak and in need of rest.

We simply stretched our hands to one another, holding on in loving silence.

Hours slipped by. Neither of us let go. We didn't need or want to.

There, in that hospital room, God held both of us in His loving arms.

There was very little I could do for my brother. Even if Lawrence had wanted to talk, grief made it difficult for me to find any words, let alone the "right" ones. I didn't know what to pray. I simply breathed Jesus' love, in and out, in and out. Jesus read the unspoken words of my heart.

And, like the air we breathe, the presence of God filled my lungs and gave me strength. In that quiet hospital room, the presence of God embraced Lawrence and me. It touched both of us. We held hands while Jesus held our hearts. I'd like to pray that He holds your heart today, dear one.

Lord, You know the one reading these words.
You know every story, every triumph and trouble.
I lift Your beloved child to You. May we both
rest in Your love today.
Whatever we face, thank You for facing it
with us. In Jesus' name, amen.

Making Space for Stillness

*While God never stops loving us, we can feel
disconnected from Him if we don't make space for Him,
if we don't take the time to be quiet, to still the chatter
and make room for His thoughts and His grace.*

BOX OF BUTTERFLIES

*We should seek God, and perhaps feel our way
toward Him and find Him. Yet He is actually not far
from each one of us.*

ADAPTED FROM ACTS 17:27, ESV

Throughout the day, I deliberately make space for God's grace. I've found that, through small intentional actions, stillness fills my heart with an awareness of God's presence and love. In the process of making tea or the gentle reminder of God's Spirit as I light a candle, I experience peace. I am centered. I know that I am loved.

There's an almost ritualistic quality to brewing tea, and—as I am an Irishwoman—a cup of tea has been my solution for everything! In making tea, there is waiting; there is quiet; there is space for grace. You must first light a flame under the kettle, then wait for it to sing. You warm the pot or the mug, measure the tea leaves or choose your favorite bag, and pour in the boiling water. As the tea steeps, you wait. God is with me in every moment of this quiet process.

And, more often than not, by the time I sit down with my steaming cup, God's peace has given me greater strength and perspective.

I also find the quiet ritual of lighting a candle draws me into stillness with God's Spirit. You'll find candles scattered throughout my home, and I light them as the day progresses. In the scratch of a match against carbon, in the *whish* as flame bursts into light, in the flicker and scent that endure, I welcome the holy presence of God. Taking the time to be still through a process like brewing tea or lighting a candle gives you a moment to pause, welcome God, and rest in His presence.

In what small but deliberate ways can you make space for grace?

When we make space for grace, we realize that God is always with us, always near. When we don't make space for grace, the chatter of the world causes us to feel disconnected. The truth is we are *not* alone, even when we feel deep loneliness; but we cannot sense God's presence or receive His peace if we overfill our lives and make no room for God.

Take a moment and ask God what small thing you might do to make space for Him today. For just a moment, be still and listen before we close in prayer.

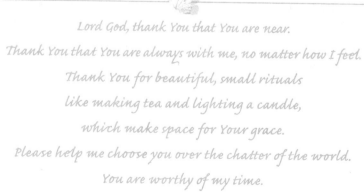

Lord God, thank You that You are near.

Thank You that You are always with me, no matter how I feel.

Thank You for beautiful, small rituals

like making tea and lighting a candle,

which make space for Your grace.

Please help me choose you over the chatter of the world.

You are worthy of my time.

In Jesus' name, amen.

Stillness in Unexpected Places

To me, a field can be just as holy as the largest cathedral.

BOX OF BUTTERFLIES

The kingdom of heaven is like treasure hidden in a field.
When a man found it, he hid it again,
and then in his joy went
and sold all he had and bought that field.

MATTHEW 13:44

Many years ago, I had my own *Field of Dreams* experience. I finally had a bit of money put by after the success of my first miniseries, *A Woman Named Jackie*. Though I owned neither car nor home in the U.S., I fancied the idea of a wee cottage in my homeland, a small corner for myself in the wide world.

Pretty soon, I was back in Ireland, wandering the rocky seashore where my father used to love walking. My dad had a quiet stillness about him, and—in the past—we would walk along the Greencastle coast in complete, easy silence, sometimes for hours. Along that very same shore, I found a small field for sale. I had no plan, but I wanted that field. I wanted it for my dad, as a way to honor his memory.

In a matter of days, I had signed the contract with a village solicitor. I drove my rented car to the field I now owned, crossing the damp ground, mud squelching over my Wellington boots. Staring across the waters of Lough Foyle, I laughed and cried, thinking, *Fine lot of good this old field is going to do me!*

Yet in the stillness of that moment, I sensed my father's joy. I also knew my Heavenly Father's presence. In that field I found not only stillness but a peace that transcends understanding.

For me, there was treasure hidden in that field. And though it looked quite the impractical purchase from all objective standpoints, I bought that field in my joy. I'm grateful that, unlike the man in Jesus' parable, I didn't sell everything I owned to purchase it (Matthew 13:44). But I did find the treasure of God's presence and healing in the stillness of that field.

The treasure of God's Kingdom *is* worth spending our all to secure—all our attention, all our time, all our resources. With these words, I'm not encouraging you to buy a literal field. I'm simply urging you to listen to God's voice and run after Him in the stillness. Don't run away from stillness; buy it up, no matter the cost.

We sometimes believe we need to find God in "official" places like church buildings. Or that we can only find peace on vacation. But if we wait for stillness to come to us, we will be waiting forever. Find your field, dear one, and allow God to make it yours in joy.

Thank You, God, for the treasure of Your presence.

Thank You for Your priceless Kingdom.

Thank You for Your peace, which passes all comprehension.

Your love is big enough to fill the whole world.

Please help me to see You everywhere, to be still with You,

to hear Your voice in the stillness.

I love You, Jesus.

Amen.

Gratitude

Gratitude Changes Our Vision

*Gratitude unlocks the fullness of life. Gratitude turns
what we have into enough, and more. It turns denial
into acceptance, chaos into order, confusion into
clarity . . . it makes sense of our past, brings peace for
today, and creates a vision for tomorrow.*

MELODY BEATTIE, *THE LANGUAGE OF LETTING GO*[51]

*"For the mountains may move and the hills disappear,
but even then My faithful love for you will remain.
My covenant of blessing will never be broken," says the
Lord, who has mercy on you.*

ISAIAH 54:10

When I returned to my brother, Lawrence's, hospital room the day after holding his hand in silence, he seemed livelier . . . perhaps even chipper. I was thrilled to see a light in his eyes and a gentle smile playing on his lips.

"Roma," he began, beckoning me over and gesturing toward the window. "These hills must have been here yesterday, but I didn't see them. Aren't they lovely?"

Indeed, they were.

The hills didn't move, but Lawrence's heart had. Lawrence once again had eyes open to the beauty around him. Though his circumstances hadn't changed dramatically, his vision had.

I am so grateful that God never changes. His faithful love is always with us. His covenant promises will never be broken, and His mercies never fail. The Bible tells us that His mercies are new every morning; great is His faithfulness.

Sometimes we lose track of God's nearness and goodness, though, don't we? We become tired, weighed down, worried. We face battles too great for us. As Lawrence fought throat cancer, he—quite understandably—lost sight of the hills.

Over years of walking with God, I've discovered that nothing restores our spiritual sight as effectively as gratitude. Gratitude for the rolling hills outside a hospital window. Gratitude for a hand to hold in silence. Gratitude for the hope of a heavenly home where no sickness, no fear, neither sorrow nor death exists.

Gratitude may not eliminate chaos, but it can make sense of our struggles in a miraculous way. Gratitude does not erase confusion but can bring clarity from within it. Gratitude enables us to see the past from God's perspective, face the present with Christ's hope, and look to the future with our Father's vision.

Colossians 4:2 urges us to "Devote yourselves to prayer, being watchful and thankful." Gratitude involves an alertness of mind, a vision for what surrounds us, and a commitment to prayer. In our loving Father's hands, these lead to a peace that surpasses human understanding.

Truly, gratitude unlocks the fullness of life. I'd like to pray for us to enjoy that fullness today.

Father, thank You that Your love never fails.
You never break Your promises.
Because of You, we can be grateful . . . always.
Life often hurts. We need You every moment.
Please open our eyes to see You in all things.
May gratitude be our first response to You.
And please help us to encourage others
to live gratefully, too.
In Jesus' name, amen.

Gratitude Defeats Anxiety

*As we express our gratitude, we must never forget
that the highest appreciation is not to utter words
but to live by them.*

JOHN F. KENNEDY[52]

*Don't worry about anything; instead, pray about
everything. Tell God what you need, and thank Him for all
He has done. Then you will experience God's peace, which
exceeds anything we can understand. His peace will guard
your hearts and minds as you live in Christ Jesus.
And now, dear brothers and sisters, one final thing.
Fix your thoughts on what is true, and honorable, and
right, and pure, and lovely, and admirable. Think about
things that are excellent and worthy of praise. Keep
putting into practice all you learned and received from
me—everything you heard from me and saw me doing.
Then the God of peace will be with you.*

PHILIPPIANS 4:6–9

COVID-19 changed all our lives.
Some experienced inconvenience; others faced death.
None of it was fair. Very little made sense. Anxiety seemed
to envelop humanity.

As days slid into weeks, which tumbled into months, God continually reminded me that prayer was the only path forward. My beloved Heavenly Father invited me, as the words from Philippians 4 record, to tell Him what I need. I'm so grateful that "Help us" prayers are blessed by the Lord and received to His heart.

Our good Father also invites us to thank Him for all He has done. This, God promises, unlocks a peace that will guard our hearts and minds. Gratitude transforms us into people who can *live* as Jesus lived.

Mark and I are empty nesters with three adult children, and we never imagined that any of them would live at home again, yet during COVID-19 we saw more of everyone. We even had Reilly's older half sister, Vanessa, and Vanessa's young son, Ocean, with us for a time. I'm thankful for the time we had together, hunkered down and slowed down. Each of us typically lives a unique and busy life, so the days of togetherness were a priceless gift.

Still, on the news, on every social media platform, all around us were triggers for worry. As a family, we chose to fix our thoughts elsewhere. We chose to put into practice what the Bible reveals. And the peace of God came with the discipline of gratitude.

As we ate dinner together almost every night, we encouraged one another to keep a grateful perspective. Each of us would share "the rose in our day," something for which we could all be grateful. It was almost as if the fragrance of a lovely flower released joy and peace into our home.

When we speak grateful words and—even more—live grateful lives, everything changes even if nothing changes. Look for the rose in your life today, dear one. And give Him thanks when you see it.

Beloved Father, You are so good.
Thank You that, no matter what happens,
we can choose to thank You.
Thank You for the peace that comes
as we give thanks.
Please help us to fix our thoughts on You, Lord.
May we see and celebrate the beauty You place
in our life today.
In Jesus' name, amen.

Gratitude Becomes a Habit

I find when I attach an attitude to an action—
something I am bound to do throughout the day—it
helps me remember the attitude more.

BOX OF BUTTERFLIES

Rejoice always, pray continually, give thanks in all
circumstances; for this is God's will for you in Christ Jesus.

1 THESSALONIANS 5:16–18

Habit [hab-it], *noun: an acquired behavior pattern*
regularly followed until it has become almost involuntary.

What are you in the habit of doing, dear one?

Growing up in Ireland, where a cup of tea is the solution for everything, I developed the habit of tea drinking. I've cultivated the habit of getting out in nature every morning, spending time hiking in the hills or strolling along the shore. God has also taught me to develop habits of gratitude.

Every morning when I get out of bed and my first foot hits the floor, I say, "Thank." Then the other foot hits the floor, and I say, "You." And all the way into the bathroom, I am whispering, "Thank You. Thank You. Thank You." A pitter-patter of gratitude as I begin my day.

I began this practice when I was filming *Touched by an Angel*. I don't remember where I read or heard about it, but as soon as I discovered this practice I knew it was something I wanted to integrate into my daily routine. I've done it ever since.

I've now added another routine to remind me to give thanks. Each time I wash my hands and feel the water run over my skin, I say it again: "Thank You. Thank You, God." It helps me take a step back from whatever is happening to remember my blessings. It's a reminder for me to acknowledge God. And so, every time I wash my hands, my perception of whatever is going on around me instantly changes.[53]

An attitude of gratitude doesn't happen by accident. It must be acquired, like a habit, by regular repetition until it becomes almost involuntary. That's why I've chosen to attach an attitude of gratitude to small, specific actions throughout my day. This practice enables me to follow Paul's instructions to "give thanks in all circumstances" (1 Thessalonians 5:18). Thanking God for simple things like waking up and having clean water to wash my hands primes my heart to be grateful for bigger things and even for challenges that stretch my faith.

What about you? I invite you to take a moment and ask God to reveal one habit to which you can attach an attitude of gratitude. Let's pray about that now.

Heavenly Father, there is so much to thank You for . . .
I'm grateful for Your love, for hope, for the home that
awaits me in heaven. I want to be grateful no matter
what happens today.
Would You please show me one action to which I can
attach gratitude?
Help me not to miss anything!
Thank You, Lord, for Who You are.
In Jesus' name, amen.

Gratitude Transforms Our Suffering

To love a person is to learn the song in their heart,
and sing it to them when they have forgotten.

ATTRIBUTED TO NORWEGIAN NOVELIST ARNE GARBORG

Let all that I am praise the Lord;
with my whole heart, I will praise His holy name.
Let all that I am praise the Lord;
may I never forget the good things
He does for me.

PSALM 103:1–2

I saw how much it hurt Mark—watching his father slide, day after day, into a more distant place. Archie Burnett, a Scottish man of stalwart character, sat quietly now, staring into space with a glazed expression and detached air. Mark and I grieved as Archie's dementia advanced; eventually he needed round-the-clock care. We found a wonderful home for Archie and visited often.

I don't remember exactly when or where we heard it, but we learned that music could help Alzheimer's patients tremendously, so we loaded some of Archie's favorite songs on playlists he might enjoy. As a Scotsman, Archie loved bagpipe music, so we included plenty of that. We also threw in tunes from the '50s and '60s that we believed might remind him of happy times.

When we placed earphones on Archie and played the music, an immediate and remarkable change occurred. The glazed eyes became bright; his movements became animated. So animated, in fact, that it almost looked like Archie was conducting an invisible orchestra. He no longer stared into the mid-distance. He was with us once again.

Playing music became a regular part of our visits, and it often felt like we were stealing Archie back from an abyss. Though my father-in-law couldn't recognize his only son, and that grieved Mark deeply, Mark could play the music of his father's heart when Archie had forgotten it.

Mark and I knew that, if we allowed it, sadness over Archie's neurological disintegration could take us under. The only path through involved gratitude. We chose to be grateful for the stolen moments, the fragmented moments that music gave us with Archie. We praised God for His gift of music. We thanked Him for the scientists who discovered music's role in helping those with dementia. Instead of looking at the leaves falling from the tree, we focused on the healthy branches still there.

Archie could not remember, but Mark and I could. We could remember the great things God has done. We could thank Him. And that's what we did.

What about you, dear one? If leaves are falling rapidly off your tree or that of someone you love, will you fixate on what is lost? What might happen if you instead chose to be grateful for the branches still flourishing? Let's pray about this now.

Dear God, it hurts watching people we love suffer.
Many reading this book are going through
very hard times.
Jesus, You understand pain.
You told us that gratitude unlocks peace
and strength.
We need that, Lord, and we pray for it.
We trust You with our hurts
and we thank You for all You've done.
Amen.

Gratitude Does Immeasurably More

One time I was at a bookstore in Los Angeles doing a signing for a children's book I had written. A young woman came up to me, tears in her eyes. She told me the most remarkable story.

BOX OF BUTTERFLIES

Now to Him who is able to do immeasurably more than all we ask or imagine, according to His power that is at work within us, to Him be glory in the church and in Christ Jesus throughout all generations, for ever and ever! Amen.

EPHESIANS 3:20–21

I often pray God will use my work to touch people's lives for Him. I've prayed this with different cast and crew members, with my beloved husband as we produced TV shows and films, with my family as we served God in different capacities.

He always does beyond what I can ask or imagine . . . immeasurably more.

The young woman who approached me in the bookstore many years ago grew up in a dire situation. Some of you reading this book have experienced abuse and neglect in your home, just like this precious daughter of God. I'm so grieved—and God's heart is grieved—by the suffering in this world.

I listened as she described how despair started to suffocate her. One night, anguish and hopelessness blocked her way forward. She no longer wanted to live, filled as she was with anger and agony at the abandonment she felt as a child, the loneliness she still felt as an adult. She took a drastic step and slid down the bathroom wall, gripping bleeding wrists. In what she believed would be her final moments, she cried out to God, "Even now, there's no one here. There's no one here." She let her head sink to her knees, waiting for death to take her.

A sound split the silence. Voices from the other room. *I don't remember turning on the television*, she thought. But it *was* on, and this young woman heard my angel-character, Monica, speak a message from God:

"You are not alone. You are never alone. Don't you know that God loves you?"

Those simple yet eternally powerful words gave this young woman enough strength to stand up and call 911. She knew that message wasn't for a character in a TV show; God was speaking to her.

I listened to her story in tearful awe, then enveloped her in a hug. All I could manage was "Thank You, God. Thank You, God."

He can do beyond what we ask for or imagine when we offer ourselves to Him. You have no idea whose life you might change with the simple words "You are not alone. God loves you." Who in your life needs to hear this message today?

Lord God, thank You that we are never alone.

Thank You for loving us.

Thank You for doing immeasurably more
than we can ask for or imagine.

Please help me to speak words of life
to those who are hurting.

Please help me remember to be grateful
when I see You work.

I am grateful to be Yours, Jesus.

In Your name I pray, amen.

Gratitude Keeps Us Close

*There were times when I would call out to
Monica and say, somewhat jokingly, "Where are you
when I need you? I miss you!"*

BOX OF BUTTERFLIES

*I wait for the Lord, my whole being waits,
and in His Word I put my hope.*

PSALM 130:5

After *Touched by an Angel* wrapped, I felt so many mixed emotions. I was tremendously grateful to be at home with Reilly. No more twelve-hour days on set meant that I could spend so much more time with my daughter, and I soaked up every minute. I thanked God again and again for the gift of being a mother.

I also mourned the loss of time with my cast and crew family. I missed playing Monica, inhabiting her spirit. She taught me so much, making me a better friend, a better listener, a more faithful servant. Playing her brought out the best in me, and I could never thank God enough for that.

Some days, as I waited for God to reveal my next step, I felt a bit adrift. I knew that He wanted me to wait patiently and confidently for projects that would bring light and hope to the world. I was grateful He had prepared me to do that. But I had been chasing work my whole life. Honestly, it felt scary not to work; I had to deliberately trust that space, even when waves of panic crashed over me.

Gratitude always pulled me back to God. Like a tether binding me to His heart, gratitude kept me close to my Heavenly Father.

One of the first projects I worked on after *Touched by an Angel* was an infomercial to raise awareness for the ministry I described earlier, Operation Smile. I traveled to Vietnam and worked in a mission hospital alongside the surgeons giving new life and hope to families with children born with facial anomalies. You simply can't refrain from gratitude when you see God working in such powerful, life-changing ways. I thanked God over and over for Who He is, for what He does, for His presence in our lives.

And on those days when I would laughingly cry out, "Where are you, Monica?" God would remind me that I was really calling out to *Him*. I would bow my head, so thankful that He would speak to me. I would feel Him come alongside me and say, *I'm right here; it's okay. Just sit. You don't have to be doing all the time. Just trust. You are doing enough. You are not alone. I'm right here with you.*

And I would simply say, "Thank You."

Thank You, God.

Thank You that, whether we feel adrift or adventurous,

You are with us.

Thank You that we don't have to be doing all the time.

Thank You that we can trust You as we wait.

Thank You for being right here with us.

We love You, Lord.

Thank You for loving us.

Amen.

Gratitude Stops Comparing

Comparison is the thief of joy.

ATTRIBUTED TO THEODORE ROOSEVELT

Since this is the kind of life we have chosen, the life of the Spirit, let us make sure that we do not just hold it as an idea in our heads or a sentiment in our hearts, but work out its implications in every detail of our lives. That means we will not compare ourselves with each other as if one of us were better and another worse. We have far more interesting things to do with our lives. Each of us is an original.

GALATIANS 5:25–26, MSG

Each of us is an original.

If you ask me, those six words could change the world, if only we let them.

Each of us is an original masterpiece, created by God to do more interesting things than "compare ourselves with each other as if one of us were better and another worse." Do you believe this, dear one?

If you've chosen a life in God, what the Apostle Paul calls "the life of the Spirit," this is nonnegotiable: we must go beyond mentally agreeing with God's promises and truth. We must *live them out*. And that means comparison, the thief of joy, must be stopped. May it steal our joy no longer!

God has granted me a great deal of success in the entertainment industry. No matter what I've accomplished, however, the lie of *more* and *better* can threaten. There will always be someone with more— more awards, more work, a more beautiful house or figure. I have more than I could have ever imagined, and yet there are still people with way more than me.

If I choose to see lack, if I choose to live my life in comparison, I've surrendered to the thief. My joy has been stolen.

That's why gratitude is so essential. There is simply no room for comparison within the words "Thank You." "Thank You" yields fullness; "Thank You" overflows. "Thank You" sees not lack but abundance. When we learn to say "Thank You" all the time, we not only acknowledge all we've been given but also make room for more to arrive.

In John 10:10, Jesus tells us that "the thief comes only to steal and kill and destroy; I have come that they may have life, and have it to the full." God's enemy wants to hijack your joy through comparison. Don't allow him to do this, dear one. Choose gratitude instead.

Each of us is an original. The masterpiece of your life is still being painted by your Heavenly Father. Whether the colors He's presently using are bright or dark, there is *something*—always something—for which you can thank Him. Let's do that right now.

Thank You, God, that I am an original.

Please help me believe this.

Thank You for giving me

more interesting things to do than compare myself with others.

Please help me to be on the lookout for those things every day.

I love You deeply. Thank You for loving me.

Amen.

Gratitude Responds with Hope

Gratitude helps us see the light in the darkness, the potential of healing among the sick, the hope among the hopeless. In spite of what I've lost, I haven't lost everything. Gratitude is the key.

BOX OF BUTTERFLIES

Whom have I in heaven but you?
I desire you more than anything on earth.
My health may fail, and my spirit may grow weak,
but God remains the strength of my heart;
He is mine forever.

PSALM 73:25–26, NLT

While we cannot control the circumstances of life, we can choose how we respond to them. True, our physical bodies may react to worrisome situations with anxiety—rapid heartbeat, shortened breathing, a sour feeling in the pit of our stomach. We may feel out of control, and we very well may be. Even then, we can choose how to respond. And, if we are to experience the peace and love of God, we must respond.

Viktor E. Frankl survived horrors most of us would prefer not to think about, let alone endure. During one of the darkest periods in human history, interned in Auschwitz and two other concentration camps, Frankl learned that between what happens to us and how we respond there is a space. That space provides us with the freedom and power to choose. That space is given to us by God.

Viktor Frankl discovered that, though one can lose everything, all is not lost: "Everything can be taken from man but one thing: the last of the human freedoms—to choose one's attitude in any given set of circumstances, to choose one's own way."[54]

Every one of us can choose. We can choose darkness and lack. Or we can choose light, hope, and gratitude.

In *The Hiding Place*, another Holocaust survivor, Corrie ten Boom, described how she thanked God for the swarming fleas in her barracks; they kept the Nazi guards from noticing the Bible study going on beneath their noses. Corrie taught people about God's light in a dark, dark place, surrounded by fleas.

I don't tell you these stories to shock you or shame you. I'm merely pointing out how miraculously gratitude can transform human circumstances. Gratitude truly is the key. The key to everything.

Keys unlock things—doors, jewelry boxes, treasure chests. Gratitude unlocks your heart. It unlocks your experience of God's presence and peace. Don't keep your heart locked against Him, beloved one. Open your mouth in gratitude and let God's presence flood in.

Neuroscience proves that gratitude and anxiety cannot coexist in the brain. They follow mutually exclusive neural pathways.[55] The next time you feel anxious, stop and list ten things you are grateful for; continue until you feel able to respond to your circumstances with God's peace and repeat as needed. I'll be choosing gratitude with you.

Thank You for bringing us through
our darkest times.
Whether we gain or lose everything,
please help us to choose light, hope,
and gratitude.
You empower us to respond and to choose, Lord.
Your love covers a multitude of sins.
Thank You.
I want to honor You with how I choose.
In Jesus' name, amen.

Gratitude Unlocks Your Heart

*I want to jump in and seize the moment.
I'm not locking up any rooms. Let's thank God
for every gift and use it to its fullest.*

BOX OF BUTTERFLIES

*This is the day that the Lord has made; let us
rejoice and be glad in it.*

PSALM 118:24, ESV

Did you grow up with a "good room" or "good furniture" that, as a child, you weren't supposed to touch? As a more casual attitude toward entertaining expanded, this kind of housekeeping went somewhat out of vogue; still many of us grew up with certain things or places that were "off-limits" except for special occasions. And no matter how we were raised, all of us have things we want to preserve and save.

In her "good room," my mother kept her greatest treasure: a set of fine china given to her and my father as a wedding gift. The set was expensive and luxurious, and my mom loved those delicate dishes. Lawrence and I knew not to go anywhere near the china cabinet, lest we unwittingly jostle and break one of the precious pieces.

Periodically, my mother would take out a little key, unlock the china cabinet, carefully wash and dry the dishes, then replace them with the same loving caution.

I don't remember ever using that china, but I remember the day every piece shattered.

During the height of the Troubles, Saracen armored personnel carriers would rumble through our narrow streets, causing the entire house to shake. One afternoon, as a tank approached, we felt the tremors and heard the Saracen's telltale metallic growl.

CRASH!

My mother's hand flew to her face. The china cabinet's top shelf had collapsed, smashing every single piece of my mother's china. The image of my mother, falling to her knees in tears, holding shards of her destroyed china, has never left me.

And yet I am grateful for that experience. I learned from it to enjoy everything I've been given, seizing each moment because nothing is guaranteed beyond it. I don't save things for a "good day," or lock things away to keep them safe. I use what I've been given, thanking God for everything, no matter how big or small.

An attitude of gratitude means that *every day* can be the best. This is the day that the Lord has made; let us rejoice and be glad in it! Every day can be a cause for celebration . . . the sun rose again! The glory of God fills the earth!

If you're currently locking anything away, saving it for "then," *now* is the time to open it to God. May we enjoy all He's given with the words "Thank You, God" ever on our lips.

Heavenly Father, thank You for this new day.

Your glorious beauty fills the whole earth.

I am so thankful for all You've given.

Please help me see the treasure in every day.

Help me to choose a thankful heart.

I am grateful You died to save me, Jesus.

May I honor Your sacrifice with

an attitude of gratitude.

Amen.

Gratitude and Acceptance

*Acceptance doesn't mean resignation; it means
understanding that something is what it is and that
there's got to be a way through it.*

MICHAEL J. FOX, *LUCKY MAN*[56]

*I know that my redeemer lives, and that in the end He
will stand on the earth.
And after my skin has been destroyed, yet in my flesh I
will see God.*

JOB 19:25–26

The world was shocked when Michael J. Fox announced his diagnosis with Parkinson's disease. The winsome, spunky young man who thrilled audiences in *Back to the Future* received, in his late twenties, a diagnosis usually reserved for those in their eighties. It seemed so unfair.

Just like it seems so unfair that children get leukemia, that teenagers suffer from crippling anxiety, that anyone hears the words: "I'm sorry; there's nothing we can do." I remember listening to our Cameron's diagnosis and wondering, *God, how does this fit in Your good plan?* I knew I could trust Jesus, but in that difficult moment I just couldn't see a path through the darkness yet.

Since his diagnosis Michael J. Fox has championed Parkinson's research and bravely thrived with his progressive condition. I love that he titled a book *Lucky Man*; Fox refuses to pity himself or succumb to resignation.

There really is a huge difference between acceptance and resignation, isn't there? Whether we're facing health challenges of our own or caring for an aging parent or seriously ill child, God shows us how to walk the path of acceptance and gratitude rather than slumped-shoulder resignation.

In the Bible, the book of Job isn't the easiest to read. There's so much heartache and loss. But I'm thankful God included Job's story in the Bible; it shows us that God knows and accepts us at our most desperate. Job bravely acknowledges his anger and confusion but returns to the truth again and again. "The Lord gave me what I had, and the Lord has taken it away. Praise the name of the Lord!" (Job 1:21b, NLT). Job could say this because he believed, with every fiber of his being, that His Redeemer lived. Job was going through hell on earth, but he would one day stand with God.

The path through the valley of the shadow of death is worship. The path through seasons of loss and heartbreak is gratitude. We may be tempted to become disheartened, angry, or even resigned to our situation. But if we acknowledge with gratitude the gifts God can bring us as we struggle, we can accept what is. We can trust there is a path through and God is walking there with us.

I don't want to become resigned, Lord.
I want to live alive to You in gratitude,
even when my circumstances are
difficult to accept.
It's not always clear why bad things happen.
It often feels unfair.
Thank You for promising to walk with us
no matter what.
I trust You because You are faithful.
With gratitude in my heart, help me to walk
this path with You.
Amen.

Gratitude for What Is Given

The greatest wealth is health.

ATTRIBUTED TO VIRGIL

So whether you eat or drink or whatever you do,
do it all for the glory of God.

1 CORINTHIANS 10:31

Over two thousand years ago, the Apostle Paul encouraged believers to remember that how we care for our bodies can either glorify God . . . or not. Health is a wealth that we cannot take for granted. Paul called our bodies the temple of God's Spirit. I'm so grateful that God Himself formed my body and dwells in me. This gratitude leads me to take seriously the call to care for my body.

I've made a commitment to be as healthy as God enables me to be. I'm not obsessive about food or exercise, but I am determined to care for my health and well-being. It's a way that I can live for the glory of God. I care for my body because it's a gift from God, a gift for which I am tremendously grateful. I honor the gift of my body by taking care of it.

Maybe because my own mother died young, I've focused more attentively on my health than some of my peers. Early on I learned the hard lesson that good health doesn't last forever; we can't take our bodies for granted. I used to think about how much I had lost when my mother's health failed. The older I get, however, the more I realize how much my mother lost. She never had the chance to see Lawrence and me grow and succeed. She never got to hold grandbabies in her arms. I long, one day, to hold in my arms any future grandchildren I may have. I also want to remain healthy because I enjoy the work God's given me and the purpose it's brought to my life.

What about you, dear friend? Do you view your body as the temple of God's Spirit? Are you grateful for whatever level of health and strength He's given you? Is gratitude to God prompting you to care tenderly and lovingly for your body?

I recognize that, for some, disease has stolen years of strength and health. It may feel difficult for you to imagine your body as God's precious temple; you may not know how to care for your body well. I'm so sorry if you find yourself in this situation.

One place we can all start is by choosing, as I do in my morning prayer, to honor God with the measure of health He *does* give. I know good health is not guaranteed. Whatever amount of health and strength God does give is a reason for me to be grateful. So I'm choosing gratitude and choosing to care for my body. What will you do with what He's given you?

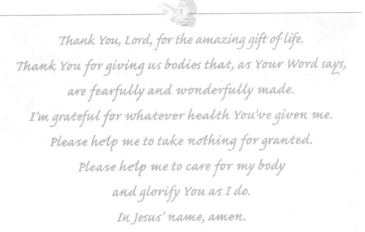

Thank You, Lord, for the amazing gift of life.
Thank You for giving us bodies that, as Your Word says,
are fearfully and wonderfully made.
I'm grateful for whatever health You've given me.
Please help me to take nothing for granted.
Please help me to care for my body
and glorify You as I do.
In Jesus' name, amen.

Gratitude for Infinite Chances

Monica: *You made the choice, Angela. You want to live.*
You just don't want to live like this.
Angela: *But I can't change the past . . . Can you?*
Monica: [Shakes her head] *But all you need to know*
about the past is that no matter what has happened,
it has all worked together to bring you to this very
moment. And it is in this moment right now that you
can choose to make everything new.

TOUCHED BY AN ANGEL, EPISODE 1.4, "FALLEN ANGELS"

Yes, God does these things again and again for people.

JOB 33:29, NLT

The cast and crew of *Touched by an Angel* loved mail day. Over the years we received tons of beautiful handwritten letters from people describing their experience watching the show, how God used it in their lives. Two groups of people seemed especially thankful for *Touched by an Angel*. Letters of gratitude from teachers and prisoners flooded in every week.

Educators told us that they used episodes to teach moral lessons. In virtually every episode, often at a crossroads in a person's life, a choice had to be made . . . a choice that could impact a person's life forever. Teachers wanted their students to learn that free will—the gift God has given each human—is something to treat reverently and gratefully, not flippantly and carelessly. They expressed gratitude for how our show helped their students grow and mature.

Prisoners, on the other hand, told us how grateful they felt watching Della's and my angel-characters, Tess and Monica, offer second—or several—chances to people who had strayed from the path of goodness. Those incarcerated for crimes they committed, those who no longer wanted to live the way that landed them in prison, discovered that, though they could not change the past, they could, in "this moment right now . . . choose to make everything new." Our viewers in prisons were so grateful for this truth, which is God's truth.

In Job 33, God reveals that He delights in offering people chance after chance to choose Him. "If there is an angel at their side, a messenger, one out of a thousand, sent to tell them how to be upright . . . then that person can pray to God and find favor with Him. They will see God's face and shout for joy; He will restore them to full well-being. And they will go to others and say, 'I have sinned, I have perverted what is right, but I did not get what I deserved. God has delivered me from going down to the pit, and I shall live to enjoy the light of life.' God does all these things to a person . . . to turn them back from the pit, that the light of life may shine on them" (Job 33:23, 26–30). How grateful I am that God is the God of infinite chances!

Wherever life finds you, whatever you've faced, today is the day to pray and find God's favor. He delights to restore you. He does not give us what we deserve but causes the light of life to shine on us. Isn't that a wonderful reason to be grateful? If you agree, let's thank Him now.

Lord, thank You for being so good and so loving.
Thank You for giving us this new day, a day
when we can turn to You and live for You.
Please heal us from the wounds of our past.
Show us every new chance You offer, that we
can walk in the light of Your love.
In Jesus' name. Amen.

Home

Your True Home

*My soul is from elsewhere. I'm sure of that,
and I intend to end up there.*

RUMI

*They were longing for a better country—a heavenly
one. Therefore God is not ashamed to be called their
God, for He has prepared a city for them.*

HEBREWS 11:16

The words of thirteenth-century poet and mystic Rumi resonate with me deeply.

Perhaps I learned, earlier than some, to look beyond this life. The loss of my mother so young and my father far before his time compelled me to search my soul. I found the love of God there. I found peace and hope. I found my true home.

Faith taught me that I would see my mother and father again. Grieving them hurt. It hurt so deeply. But in the echo of my soul, God lit a bright fire, the flames ignited by confidence that—one glorious day—I will be home with Him and with those I love. I am not of this world; I am only passing through.

I love life. I embrace it with such gratitude. The love of God for me and for all His creation stuns with joy. And yet this is not my true home. Nor is it yours. You and I were made for even more than this.

Rumi writes: "The breeze at dawn has secrets to tell you; Don't go back to sleep. You must ask for what you really want; Don't go back to sleep. People are going back and forth across the doorsill where the two worlds touch. The door is round and open. Don't go back to sleep."[57]

I suppose it's possible that Rumi wrote only of rising with the dawn and sleeping less, but I don't believe so. I sense he is calling us to be awake in God, awake to the world beyond, to the place where our world and the next meet. Don't go back to sleep, my friend. Awaken to the hope of heaven.

Hebrews 11 has been called the "Hall of Faith." It details the lives of those who bravely walked with God until they made it all the way home. "They were longing for a better country," verse 16 declares, "a heavenly one. Therefore God is not ashamed to be called their God, for He has prepared a city for them."

Your soul is from elsewhere; your true home is with God. Do you intend to go there? What would it be like if you lived with both joy and gratitude in the *now* and with the hope of heaven always before you? I believe you'd be awake. I want to be awake. What about you?

Thank You, God, for making us a glorious home in heaven.

Thank You for never being ashamed that we are Yours.

Please help us to be awake and alive, Lord.

Help us to cultivate joy, gratitude, and a hope in heaven.

We are so grateful that You are always with us.

We love You.

Amen.

A Better Home Awaits You

There are loved ones in the glory
Whose dear forms you often miss.
When you close your earthly story,
Will you join them in their bliss?
Will the circle be unbroken
By and by, by and by?
Is a better home awaiting
In the sky, in the sky?[58]

ADA R. HABERSHON, "WILL THE CIRCLE BE UNBROKEN?," 1907

"This, then, is how you should pray:
'Our Father in heaven, hallowed be Your name,
Your kingdom come, Your will be done, on earth
as it is in heaven.
Give us today our daily bread. And forgive us our debts,
as we also have forgiven our debtors.
And lead us not into temptation, but deliver us
from the evil one.'"

MATTHEW 6:9–13

I hung up the phone and booked a flight as quickly as I could. My brother, Lawrence, had very little time remaining on earth; both family and doctors recommended that, if I wished to say a final good-bye, I get to Ireland as soon as possible.

Unfortunately, flying to Ireland takes time. I had to land at London's Heathrow Airport before I could board a smaller jet bound for my home country. I anxiously phoned from Heathrow and gratefully heard that Lawrence was still alive. I wanted so badly to see him one more time and say good-bye.

After arriving in Ireland, I joined Fiona, Lawrence's wife, and Laura and Lisa, his adult daughters, at my brother's bedside. How thankful I was to be there, to get the chance to hold his hand one last time and say good-bye. I did not know if he knew I was there or not, but I thanked him for waiting for me and I encouraged him to let go and head on home.

At some point, my sister-in-law and nieces decided to join hands and pray the "Our Father." It's a beautiful prayer acknowledging God's presence and holiness, our complete dependence on Him, our need to forgive and be forgiven, the dangers that face us, and the truth that God can deliver us from evil. It's also a prayer of surrender. *Your* will be done, Father.

Each of my brother's daughters took one of his hands. His lovely wife and I closed the circle. Together, with love, with tears streaming, we prayed. And while we did, Lawrence breathed his last. It was a holy moment, one of the most beautiful, if unexpected, blessings of my life. The veil between this life and the next felt so thin.

As the hymn that opened this devotional proclaims, there are loved ones in glory we dearly miss. The circle doesn't have to be broken, though. A better home awaits you, dear one. Do you believe it?

Heavenly Father, You know exactly who
is reading this prayer.
You know whether death looks frightening
or like a trip home to them.
Thank You that You carry us as
the veil becomes thin.
We can trust You in death as we can in life.
Help us to see every unexpected blessing,
even in our loved ones going home.
In Jesus' name, amen.

As You Journey Home

If you change the way you look at things, the things you look at change.

DR. WAYNE W. DYER[59]

I keep asking that the God of our Lord Jesus Christ, the glorious Father, may give you the Spirit of wisdom and revelation, so that you may know Him better.
I pray that the eyes of your heart may be enlightened in order that you may know the hope to which He has called you . . .

EPHESIANS 1:17–18A, NLT

Even if you didn't know what it was called, you've most likely seen an ambiguous image. Also called reversible pictures, these images change based on your perspective. You may have seen *Rubin's Vase*, which looks like either an urn-shaped container or two faces gazing at one another. Or perhaps you've seen *My Wife and My Mother-in-Law*, a German sketch from the late nineteenth century that, depending on how you look at it, reveals either a beautiful young woman from a distance or an older woman in sharp relief.

Ambiguous images work with our visual processing in a fascinating way. We literally see differently based on how we perceive.

What a metaphor for life! How we experience everything between our birth and our passing into eternity can be altered by a change of perspective.

In many ways, our earthly journey is a long trip home. I've found it so essential to allow God, along the way, to show me the "other image" in my life's circumstance. If we can only see life from one angle, we become stuck . . . waylaid . . . broken down . . . a traveler whose journey has been hijacked by situation.

In Ephesians 1, the Apostle Paul offers us another option. He invites us to pray, as he does, that the eyes of our heart would be enlightened, open to God's truth and hope. Jesus calls us to surrender our perspective to Him.

One day, when we finally arrive home, we will see clearly the *both . . . and* of life. We will understand—unambiguously—the eternal reality that pervaded every part of our story. We may see incompletely and partially now, but we can always ask God to help us see more clearly as we move toward home.

Dear friend, God knows and loves you so tenderly, so deeply. Nothing can separate you from His love. If you're feeling stuck or weighed down, please join me in praying for a change of perspective. If you know someone who's struggling with seeing life from a different point of view, why not pray this for them, too?

Precious Lord God,

You know us completely. You love us completely.

Thank You!

Life can be puzzling and challenging.

We don't always know what is best or right.

We ask with humble confidence that You

grant us new perspective.

Please make our eyes focused and clear, that

we might know You more.

May our journey home to You be filled

with Your peace.

Amen.

Homeward Confidence

Baby, He's already done great things.

DELLA REESE

*Now faith is confidence in what we hope for and
assurance about what we do not see.*

HEBREWS 11:1

Certainty.

What a gift that is. To be so confident in someone or something that you speak with boldness, act with courage, face the hardships and hallelujahs in life with the same attitude.

Della Reese exemplified this kind of faith.

I'd say something like "God's going to do great things," and Della would instantly respond, "Baby, He's already done great things." I'll never forget, after kindly challenging me to open my heart to love again, Della instructing me: "Don't pray it over and over. Pray it once, and then just trust." Della *knew* that God would act; we don't have to beg Him again and again.

Even as my precious friend moved closer to her heavenly home, Della spoke words of trust and confidence. She lived in the certainty that she was loved by her Eternal Father (Jeremiah 31:3), carried by Jesus (Isaiah 40:11), and sealed by His Spirit (Ephesians 1:13).

Della's faith moved mountains. Della's faith moved me.

I don't always feel certain. I can honestly relate to Jesus' disciple

Thomas, who experienced doubt and confusion (John 20:24–31). I have often reflected on how most people have Thomas moments throughout life. We want to see evidence, not exercise the certainty of faith. Gratefully, we don't all feel like Thomas at the same time!

Having a friend with faith as great as Della's was a priceless gift. I miss her every day. But I also carry with me the certainty and confidence in God that Della built in me.

Most of us don't look forward to death. Even if, as believers in Jesus, we don't *fear* death, we're usually not eager for its arrival. I watched Della walk toward her heavenly home with her heart and head held high. She knew—without a shadow of doubt—that her best days were ahead of her.

Indeed, Della set an example of extraordinary strength even in her death. I have no doubt that her faith was the secret of her confidence and peace in the final moments of life. We all need an example like Della, an example of bold faith and certainty. The people around us profoundly influence our lives. Our faith is shaped by those around us.

Who is currently influencing you? If you don't have a friend with unshakable faith, why not ask God for one? And perhaps you can become this kind of friend for someone else.

Heavenly Father, You are trustworthy and true.

We love You!

Thank You for the great gift of friendship.

Thank You for people who set an example of certainty in You.

Please help us to receive the unexpected blessing

of a friend full of faith until the very end.

We trust You with our lives, Lord.

In Jesus' name, amen.

There's No Place Like Home

*No matter how dreary and gray our homes are, we . . .
would rather live there than in any other country, be it
ever so beautiful. There is no place like home.*

L. FRANK BAUM, *THE WONDERFUL WIZARD OF OZ*[1]

*The fruit of that righteousness will be peace;
its effect will be quietness and confidence forever.
My people will live in peaceful dwelling places,
in secure homes,
in undisturbed places of rest.*

ISAIAH 32:17–18

In 1900, L. Frank Baum published a novel whose heroine, Dorothy, became one of the most cherished characters of all time. In the 1939 cinematic version of Baum's tale, Judy Garland brought Dorothy to life in vibrant Technicolor, and the words "There's no place like home" echoed in homes across the world.

Undoubtedly, Baum's story is marvelous. The film is spectacular, still considered a classic example of moviemaking magic, well over eighty years later. But I believe there's something deeper and truer that we respond to in this tale.

Dorothy's words reflect both a *spiritual hope* and an *eternal reality* belonging to every human heart. Truly, *there is no place like home.*

The latter half of Isaiah 32 foretells a day of promise, a day when the troubles of this world will fade forever, when God's peace will fill all the land. Then, the prophet pronounces, God's people will live in "secure homes, in undisturbed places of rest." Isn't it breathtakingly beautiful to know there is a home awaiting us, a home of undisturbed peace and confidence? There is no place on earth like this because there is no place like our eternal home.

In the Land of Oz, Dorothy comes to the slow realization that, no matter how far she's run, no matter how grim the circumstances, the home she seeks has always been as near as her very breath. We're so much like Dorothy, who thought she needed certain things to make her whole and get her back home. We're like her companions—the Scarecrow, the Tin Man, and the Cowardly Lion—who believed they needed a brain, a heart, and courage. "If only, if only, if only . . . ," each character cries throughout the book. But when Dorothy finally arrives at home, she realizes that what she truly needed has been with her all along.

Beloved child of God, what you need is with you right now. The longings of your heart for peace and rest, for confidence and security—indeed *all human longings*—point to the ultimate yearning for our hearts to be, finally and forever, at home with God. God Himself is our home, more than a place or a thing or a time, so let's make ourselves at home in Him today.

Thank You, God, for the promise of home.
Thank You for the promise of peace
and confidence.
Thank You for the hope that keeps us going,
especially on days when life seems
dreary and gray.
You are near to us every moment.
We can make ourselves at home in You . . .
thank You!
Please help us to live at home in Your love.
In Jesus' name, amen.

Longing for Home

I found a Welsh word the other day that I had never come across before: hiraeth. *It is defined as a homesickness for a home to which you cannot return, a home that maybe never was; the nostalgia, the yearning, the grief for the lost places of your past.*

BOX OF BUTTERFLIES

Samuel took a stone and set it up between Mizpah and Shen. He named it Ebenezer, saying, "Thus far the Lord has helped us."

1 SAMUEL 7:12

When was the last time you felt homesick? Were you separated from your family and longing to return? Was it way back in your childhood, perhaps when you went to camp or to school? Maybe you feel homesick now, though you can't pinpoint why.

I've experienced homesickness for a great deal of my life. When I came across the Welsh term *hiraeth*, I responded as a girl whose childhood essentially ended at age ten when her mother's bright light was taken from this world. I've carried a longing for that home ever since . . . the home that was filled with laughter and joy and a mother's love. For all I've been given, I still long. I long for my mom and dad. I long for Reilly to meet them. I long too for Mark, James, and Cameron to meet them too. I long to share stories with my parents of where life has taken me.

What can I do with this longing, this void in me that can only be filled by God, that will only be healed when I make it all the way home to heaven?

God gives us a tender and loving answer. Through the practice of setting up stones of remembrance, God taught the Israelites—and He teaches us—to remember with our eyes on Him. In 1 Samuel, God instructs the prophet to set up an *Ebenezer*, which means "stone of help." Every time they looked at that stone, God wanted His people to remember "Thus far the Lord has helped us" (1 Samuel 7:12).

When I wrote *Box of Butterflies*, it was—in many ways—my stone of remembrance. With each word, I set up a monument to God's faithfulness. I traced His fingerprints on every part of my life story. It hurt to remember some things, but my *hiraeth*—my heartache for the home that was—diminishes as my homesickness for heaven increases.

Not all of us write books, but all of us can set up stones of remembrance. Perhaps you have prayer journals or scrapbooks tracing God's presence throughout your life. Maybe you've composed music or created visual art? If you don't currently have a stone of remembrance, maybe now is the time?

As you ponder these things, let's use the words of the wonderful hymn "Come Thou Fount of Every Blessing" as a prayer:

"Here I raise my Ebenezer;
Hither by Thy help I'm come;
And I hope, by Thy good pleasure,
Safely to arrive at home.
Jesus sought me when a stranger,
Wandering from the fold of God;
He, to rescue me from danger,
Interposed His precious blood."
Thank You, Lord. Forever thank You.
Amen.

Remembering Home

*When we awaken fully to God, it's as if we finally
remember that we are not merely caterpillars but that
we are, in fact, beautiful butterflies with wings to fly.*

BOX OF BUTTERFLIES

*Therefore, if anyone is in Christ, he is a new creation.
The old has passed away; behold, the new has come.*

2 CORINTHIANS 5:17, ESV

When God adopted us as His beloved children, something incredible occurred. We were transformed . . . made new. The old passed away and new life began. What joy!

We don't always *feel* that newness of life, though, do we? We get sidetracked or confused. The weight of life causes us to forget who we are. Like the Prodigal Son Jesus described in Luke 15, we start making ourselves at home in the pigpen. Our true home is with the Father, though, and He doesn't want us to forget it.

Gerald May was a brilliant theologian and psychiatrist who helped people surrender their thoughts—many of which were automatically and repetitively negative—to the healing truth of God. May observed that "human spiritual longing is, finally, the humility of realizing that we have forgotten who we are . . . There can be times in the process of seeking that we are reassured that however much we are searching, we are at some level even more devoutly being searched for . . . that in fact we have already been found."[61]

What would happen if your child got lost and couldn't remember the way home? Or worse, couldn't remember who they are? What would it be like to watch a precious son or daughter strive and stress—inching through life like a caterpillar—never stretching their God-given wings to soar?

I imagine God often looks on us, His dearly loved children, with the tenderness and compassion we would have for a child who forgot, a child who didn't understand that they were made to fly.

Our Heavenly Father isn't angry that we often forget who we are, that we search and seek. But the truth is we've already been found. We've already been made new. We are not earthbound. We can and will soar with God if we only stretch our wings.

If you've forgotten who you are—or perhaps you've never really known—today is the day to reach out to your Heavenly Father's loving arms. You'll find that He's been scanning the horizon for you all along, waiting for you just like the father in Jesus' prodigal son parable. He can't wait to welcome you, to give you rest, and to remind you who you are.

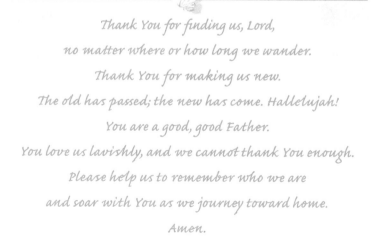

Thank You for finding us, Lord,
no matter where or how long we wander.
Thank You for making us new.
The old has passed; the new has come. Hallelujah!
You are a good, good Father.
You love us lavishly, and we cannot thank You enough.
Please help us to remember who we are
and soar with You as we journey toward home.
Amen.

Home but Not Home

If I find in myself a desire which no experience in this world can satisfy, the most probable explanation is that I was made for another world.

C. S. LEWIS, *MERE CHRISTIANITY*[62]

[You] are not of the world, just as I am not of the world.

JOHN 17:16, ESV

What do you want out of life? What do you *really* want? Many of us have some kind of answer at the ready: "I want to be happy," "to be healthy," to get through *this*, avoid *that*, have X, or get rid of Y.

According to C. S. Lewis, "Most people, if they had really learned to look into their own hearts, would know that they do want, and want acutely, something that cannot be had in this world. There are all sorts of things in this world that offer to give it to you, but they never quite keep their promise."

We think losing those ten pounds will finally make us feel better about ourselves. We believe if our children were settled in good marriages with sweet kids, we'd be happy, too. We wonder why that purchase or that sale didn't quite make us feel the way we hoped it would.

The reason is because our longings—our most acute longings—reveal that we are made for another world: a world of perfect peace and joy, a world without a single sorrow. Our true home is with Jesus, and we are all on a journey home.

The sweetest pleasures we experience in this life were never meant to satisfy, but only increase our hunger. *We are in the world, but not made for it.*

Lewis concludes: "I must take care, on the one hand, never to despise, or be unthankful for, these earthly blessings, and on the other, never to mistake them for the something else of which they are only a kind of copy, or echo, or mirage. I must keep alive in myself the desire for my true country, which I shall not find till after death; I must never let it get snowed under or turned aside; I must make it the main object of life to press on to that other country and to help others to do the same."[63]

Press on with me, dear one. Let's not get snowed under or turned aside. And let's make it our aim to help others keep their eyes fixed on the true prize, our eternal home. May we be thankful for every earthly blessing, and journey toward home together.

Heavenly Father,

Thank You for making this beautiful earth.

There is so much here to enjoy—sunrises, sunsets,

the laughter of children,

the sweet summer breeze on my face,

and the crisp bite of fall.

Thank You for promising to fulfill our longings.

Please help us to enjoy and thank You for

every earthly blessing while pressing on to our true home.

And please help us to reach out to others, in Your love.

Amen.

At Home in Thin Moments

The veil between this world and the next is just that, a thin veil. We are closer than we think, though we may feel so far. Separation is just an illusion.

BOX OF BUTTERFLIES

Jesus told her, "I am the resurrection and the life. Anyone who believes in Me will live, even after dying."

JOHN 11:25, NLT

I don't really believe in coincidence. Coincidence, it's been said, is God's way of remaining anonymous. Now *that* I can get behind.

If we live with eyes peeled, looking for how beautiful things come together in a way that shows there is a good plan, that something bigger is always going on, and that God is at work, I believe life becomes truer, fuller, and deeper.

Either there is no God or there is only God.

And there is only God.

Sometimes, as we journey toward our heavenly home, we must look intently for "God-incidences." Other times God's fingerprints are so obvious we can only laugh and thank Him joyfully. These moments remind us that the veil between heaven and earth is much thinner than we often believe.

The Celtic people, many of whom lived in my home country,

Ireland, used the phrase "thin space" to identify a location where earth and heaven touch in a special way. I have experienced "thin moments" in my life, times when the separation between this life and the next sheds its illusion.

In thin moments, God uses butterflies to remind me that, because Jesus is the resurrection and the life (present tense), my mother *lives*. Please allow me to tell you the story of one such thin moment.

I once won a gala raffle after only having purchased two tickets. In a giant pool, both my tickets were drawn. The prize? A piece from jewelry designer Thanh Hoang. Thanh showed me exquisite work from her Le Dragon d'Or collection. But she also told me she had one piece, made fifteen years ago, that no one ever bought. "It is an unusual piece," she confessed, "but as I was leaving this morning, I had a strong feeling that I should bring it." She pulled out a stunning butterfly ring.

I could have called this coincidence, but I don't believe it was. I believe that God gave me this precious thin moment to remind me that my mom is near, safe in His presence and waiting with Him for my arrival home.

If we believe what Jesus declared in John 11:25—that He is the resurrection and the life, that we will live after we die—then the world is a lot thinner than we imagine. May we be on the lookout for thin spaces and thin moments with Him today and every day.

Thank You, Lord Jesus,
for dying and being raised back to life.
Thank You for being the Living God,
the everlasting God.
Thank You that I will live with You
forever in paradise.
While I'm still here on earth,
please help me to see and celebrate You
everywhere.
I love You, Lord.
Amen.

His Masterpiece, His Home

We are surrounded by poetry on all sides . . .

VINCENT VAN GOGH[64]

*For we are God's masterpiece. He has created us anew
in Christ Jesus, so we can do the good things He planned
for us long ago.*

EPHESIANS 2:10, NLT

I didn't always know that I would be an actress. I enjoyed acting,
but I didn't know how I'd make a living out of it. So, I did something far more practical . . . I went to art school. That was my
idea of a viable career; I smile at the memory.

God had given me the ability to draw and paint what I dreamed.
Because I excelled in art from an early age, I received affirmation
from others. When I settled in at art school, things progressed well. I
immersed myself in color, paint, and beauty. I loved not only the art
but also the letters of Vincent van Gogh. In one, to his brother Theo,
he describes *becoming* the paint, not merely painting.

Through extracurricular activities, I found myself drawn to become the paint more and more. Acting seemed the best way to do
that. God began directing my steps down this new path, and I jour-
neyed with Him because I trusted Him. His Word told me, as He
tells us, that He has beautiful things for us to do, planned long ago.

Ephesians 2:10 also reveals that each one of us is a masterpiece created by God. The Greek word used here, *poiema*—from which we get our English word "poem"—means nothing less than an incomparable work of genius. God, the Great Artist, designed you perfectly. He is painting the canvas of your life. He made you the paint that reveals His beauty and glory to the world.

Van Gogh claimed that "we are surrounded by poetry on all sides," and Ephesians 2 certainly affirms this. God's *poiéma*, His masterpiece, surrounds you; indeed, it is coming to fullness in and through you, dear one.

You don't have to be an artist by profession or even hobby to become the paint in God's hands. You only need to surrender to Him. Instead of trying to paint your own life, hand over the brush. The masterpiece He has designed and is creating in you far surpasses what you could imagine or dream.

It's true; we won't see the full beauty of who we are until we make it all the way home. Some liken the unfinished quality of our lives to an intricate tapestry. The beautifully woven image looks whole and complete from one side; on the reverse, however, lies a tangle of thread and color that hardly appears artistic, let alone a masterpiece.

No matter what the tapestry of your life presently looks like, I promise—because *God promises*—that He is making something beautiful in His time.

Heavenly Father, You are beautiful
beyond description.
You create all things well, including us.
You tell us that we are Your masterpieces.
Please help us to believe this and live this truth.
May Your beauty be on display through us.
When we lose hope, please remind us that
what we see is not finished.
We trust You with the paintbrush, Lord.
Amen.

You'll Never Walk Alone

No Matter What

Our lives probably look very different—yours and mine.
But I know that we all share one thing in common, and
that is that our Father in heaven loves each of us equally
and fiercely. He is forging a beautiful butterfly out of
whatever cocoon you may be enduring.

BOX OF BUTTERFLIES

"Fear not, for I have redeemed you;
I have called you by name, you are Mine.
When you pass through the waters, I will be with you;
and through the rivers, they shall not overwhelm you;
when you walk through fire you shall not be burned,
and the flame shall not consume you.
For I am the Lord your God,
the Holy One of Israel, your Savior."

ISAIAH 43:1B–3A, ESV

None of us traverses the same path, but every one of us walks through the fire at some point. Every one of us feels overwhelmed at some point, as if the floodwaters of life will drown us. I imagine that, could the caterpillar speak, it would cry out as the very silk cocoon it was designed to weave envelops it in darkness. I can almost hear the sound of struggle a caterpillar would make, breaking free from the cocoon in which its wings formed. We are not unlike the caterpillar. Often, we are formed in darkness and struggle.

I don't know what trouble you have faced or may currently be facing. I don't know how hot the fire or how high the waves in your life. But I do know the One Who walks with you. Isaiah promises that He is walking you *through*, beloved one. You are not alone. Never alone. You have been called by name and chosen. You are His, and He will never leave you. "In this world you will have trouble," Jesus affirmed. "But take heart! I have overcome the world" (John 16:33).

The song my mother sang to me every night before her passing came from the Rodgers and Hammerstein musical *Carousel*. When I was a child, listening to my mother's beautiful voice singing "You'll Never Walk Alone" reminded me that, even after she put me to bed, she was somehow still with me. After her death that song came to symbolize even more. And then, years later, I heard the theme song for *Touched by an Angel*, "Walk with You," which told the story that—no matter what—there is Someone by your side.

Our God is a no-matter-what God. How I thank Him for that truth.

No matter what you go through, God walks with you.

No matter how alone you feel, your feelings don't always tell you the truth. You never, never walk alone.

Thank You, Lord, for being
a no-matter-what Savior.
Thank You for walking with us through every fire.
Thank You that, no matter how high the waves get,
You are higher and stronger still.
Thank You for Your never-failing love.
I love You, Lord.
I want to walk with You more closely.
Help me to do that, in Jesus' name.
Amen.

Welcome the Dawn

Take heart. Have faith. And when the light comes, as it always does, enjoy the flight to the rest of your life.

BOX OF BUTTERFLIES

When Jesus spoke again to the people, He said, "I am the Light of the World. Whoever follows Me will never walk in darkness, but will have the light of life."

JOHN 8:12

I've always loved the words of Bengali poet Rabindranath Tagore, who once wrote: "Death is not extinguishing the light; it is only putting out the lamp as dawn has come." Tagore wrote these words in 1902, after losing both his wife and daughter. Over the next five years, Tagore watched his father and then his eleven-year-old son die, too.[65] I can only imagine his grief. And yet this wise man spoke and wrote of death as "dawn," the awakening of light, not the end of it.

When Jesus came to the world, as the Light of the World, He made darkness a choice. We do not *have* to live in darkness any longer. Light has come. Even death—the great enemy—has lost its sting. We need have no fear. We can welcome the dawn.

As I mentioned earlier, Mark and I named our production company LightWorkers Media. We believe that Light has come and He will be with us forever. The Light of the World, Jesus Christ, dwells in us when we receive His love and forgiveness. Darkness has dominion over us no longer.

John 8:12 promises that whoever follows Jesus "will never walk in darkness, but will have the light of life." This verse begs a question, though: Are you following Jesus? Are you walking with Him? If you want to deliberately walk apart from Him, you can distance yourself. He will never walk away, but you can move yourself further and further from His light if you choose to do that.

I urge you, dear friend, to walk in the light. To walk closely *with* the Light of the World. This is where I choose to be, and I pray you will choose that, too. When we walk in the light, we discover that we are not bound to this earth forever. We were made to soar.

Take heart. Have faith. And when the light comes, as it always does, enjoy the flight to the rest of your life.

Light of the World, You extinguished the darkness.

Thank You!

You welcome us into the light of Your love.

Thank You!

You expel fear and bring peace.

Thank You!

I long to walk in You and with You.

Please teach me Your ways.

I love You and I want to love You more.

May Your light shine through me, for all the world to see.

In Jesus' name, amen.

I'll See You at Home

May the road rise up to meet you,
May the wind be always at your back.
May the sun shine warm upon your face,
The rains fall soft upon your fields, and,
Until we meet again,
May God hold you in the palm of His hand.

TRADITIONAL IRISH BLESSING

You make known to me the path of life;
in Your presence there is fullness of joy;
at Your right hand are pleasures forevermore.

PSALM 16:11, ESV

A s our ninety-day journey together comes to a close, this is my prayer: "May God hold you in the palm of His hand." The palm of God's hand . . . a place of safety and intimacy, of love and protection. This is the peace to which I commit you in prayer.

The Bible references God's hand quite often. Indeed, Isaiah 49:16 makes a startling claim. "See, I have written your name on the palms of My hands," God declares. The Hebrew word *chaqaq*, translated here as "written," is a beautifully nuanced term. It means "engraved," "carved," or "cut in," as a dwelling place might be cut into stone, or a monument carved as a lasting reminder.[66]

You are engraved on the palm of God's hand. He will never forget you. He willingly wrote you there because He loves you. He carved out a place of forever-safety for you. You are held, at home, in the palm of His hand.

There, Psalm 16:11 promises, "are pleasures forevermore." In God's presence "is fullness of joy." That's why I pray the blessing of my homeland for you, that God might hold you in the palm of His hand. Not only is it the right and the safest place to be; it's also the place of abundant life and joy. There is no place like home.

Our journey through this devotional may be at an end, but I know that, one day, we will meet. It may or may not be on this earth. But I know we will meet in heaven. I'll see you there.

I'll see you at home.

Lord God, thank You for this journey.

Thank You for Your Word of life, light, and truth.

Thank You for engraving our names on the palms of Your hands.

Thank You that with You is the path of life.

Thank You that pleasure and fullness of joy are at Your right hand.

Please help me to take all that I've learned through this journey

and live differently because of who You are and Whose I am.

I am Yours forever.

In Jesus' name, amen.

Endnotes

1. Roma Downey, *Box of Butterflies: Discovering the Unexpected Blessings All around Us* (Brentwood, TN: Howard Books, 2018), 14–15, Kindle.
2. Ibid., 18.
3. Ibid., 19.
4. "Compassion," accessed July 14, 2021, at https://www.dictionary.com/browse /compassion.
5. Downey, *Butterflies,* 20–21.
6. Matthew 6:22, NASB.
7. John Couwels, "Passenger Forced to Land Plane Meets His 'Co-pilots,'" CNN.com, March 31, 2010, accessed August 13, 2021, at http://www.cnn .com/2010/TRAVEL/03/29/couwels.emergency.landing/index.html.
8. Ibid., and Staff Writer, "Passenger Landed Plane with 'Focused Fear,'" CNN.com, April 14, 2009, accessed August 13, 2021, at https://www.cnn .com/2009/US/04/14/plane.emergency/index.html.
9. Downey, *Butterflies*, 21.
10. Adapted from "The Serenity Prayer" by Reinhold Niebuhr, 1951, accessed July 15, 2021, at https://en.wikipedia.org/wiki/Serenity_Prayer.
11. Ray Josephs, "Robert Frost's Secret," *Cincinnati Enquirer*, "This Week Magazine," September 5, 1954, 2, column 1, accessed August 11, 2021, at https:// quoteinvestigator.com/2018/04/01/life-goes/#return-note-18269-1.
12. Winston Churchill, from a speech to the Canadian Parliament, Ottawa, December 30, 1941, accessed August 11, 2021, at https://winstonchurchill.org /resources/quotes/famous-quotations-and-stories/.
13. Rick Warren, *The Purpose Driven Life: What on Earth Am I Here For?* (Grand Rapids, MI: Zondervan, 2012), 21.
14. Downey, *Butterflies*, 25.
15. Ibid., 44.
16. Ibid., 142.
17. Fred Rogers, "Having People Close Can Calm Child's Fears," *Orlando Sentinel*, originally published June 25, 1986, summary and explanation available

at https://interviews.televisionacademy.com/interviews/fred-rogers, in a televised interview in which Rogers retells this story and expands on his 1986 newspaper column, accessed August 3, 2021.

18. Adapted from Downey, *Butterflies*, 83.

19. Ibid., 59.

20. Ibid., 186.

21. Downey, *Butterflies*, 63.

22. Ibid., 60.

23. Ibid., 61.

24. Adapted from Downey, *Butterflies*, 73–74.

25. Ibid., 138.

26. All preceding paragraphs adapted from Downey, *Butterflies*, 78–81.

27. Ibid., 86.

28. Adapted from Downey, *Butterflies*, 86–87.

29. This paragraph and the preceding taken and/or adapted from Downey, *Butterflies*, 88–89.

30. Downey, *Butterflies*, 89.

31. This paragraph and the preceding taken and/or adapted from Downey, *Butterflies*, 90–91.

32. Ibid., 99.

33. Downey, *Butterflies*, 98.

34. Ibid., 105.

35. Michael Chekhov, *Michael Chekhov's Lessons for Teachers: Expanded Edition*, transcribed and translated into English by Jessica Cerullo from the original shorthand notes by Deirdre Hurst du Prey, edited by Jessica Cerullo (New York: Light Rail, 2018), lesson 27.

36. Dallas Willard, *The Divine Conspiracy: Rediscovering Our Hidden Life in God* (San Francisco, CA: Harper, 1998), 12, and Dallas Willard, *Life without Lack: Living in the Fullness of Psalm 23* (Nashville, TN: Thomas Nelson, 2018).

37. Downey, *Butterflies*, 116.

38. Ibid., 33–34.

39. All preceding paragraphs adapted from Downey, *Butterflies*, 66–68.

40. Downey, *Butterflies*, 112.

41. Ibid., 113.

42. Irenaeus, *Adversus Haereses* (Against Heresies), book 4, chapter 20, paragraph 7.

43. Antoine de Saint-Exupéry, *Wind, Sand and Stars*, translated by Lewis Galantière (New York: Harcourt, 2002), 215.

44. Downey, *Butterflies*, 122.

45. Ibid., 132.

46. Quoted in Downey, *Butterflies*, 155–156.

47. Henri Nouwen, *You Are the Beloved: Daily Meditations for Spiritual Living*, entry for January 3.

48. Ibid., 149.

49. Ibid., 150.

50. See Isaiah 30, Hebrew Interlinear Text, accessed August 16, 2021, at https://biblehub.com/interlinear/isaiah/30.htm.

51. Melody Beattie, *The Language of Letting Go* (Center City, MN: Hazelden, 1990), 218.

52. John F. Kennedy, "Thanksgiving Proclamation," White House Lawn, November 18, 1963, transcript accessed July 23, 2021, at https://www.presidency.ucsb.edu/documents/proclamation-3560-thanksgiving-day-1963.

53. Downey, *Butterflies*, 173–174.

54. Viktor E. Frankl, *Man's Search for Meaning* (1959; repr., Boston, MA: Beacon Press, 2006), 66.

55. Dan Baker, Ph.D., and Cameron Stauth, *What Happy People Know: How the New Science of Happiness Can Change Your Life for the Better* (New York: St. Martin's Press, 2003), 81.

56. Quote excerpted from Fox's book *Lucky Man* for "Michael J. Fox at 50: 'I Don't Look at Life as a Battle,'" Parade.com, March 29, 2012, accessed August 20, 2021, at https://parade.com/40559/dotsonrader/michael-j-fox-excerpt/ .

57. Quoted by Paulo Coelho in "Rumi's Wisdom," *Stories & Reflections* (blog), accessed August 17, 2021, at https://paulocoelhoblog.com/2015/10/02/character-of-the-week-rumi/.

58. Ada R. Habershon, "Will the Circle Be Unbroken?" (1907), Hymn 55 in Charles M. Alexander, *Alexander's Gospel Songs No. 2* (New York: Fleming H. Revell, 1910).

59. Wayne W. Dyer, "Success Secrets," *Wayne's Blog*, accessed August 16, 2021, at https://www.drwaynedyer.com/blog/success-secrets/.

60. L. Frank Baum, *The Wonderful Wizard of Oz*, illustrated edition (Orinda, CA: SeaWolf Press, 2019), 29.

61. Gerald May, *Will and Spirit: A Contemplative Psychology* (San Francisco, CA: Harper & Row, 1982), 89.

62. C. S. Lewis, *Mere Christianity* (New York: HarperCollins), 2015, 135.

63. Ibid., 136–137.

64. In a letter to his brother Theo, dated March 21–28, 1883, full text accessed August 16, 2021, at http://www.webexhibits.org/vangogh/letter/12/276.htm?qp=feelings.love.

65. Quoted in Shuvra Dey, "Death Is Not Extinguishing the Light; It Is Putting Out the Lamp As Dawn Has Come—Rabindranath Tagore," GetBengal.com, August 8, 2020, accessed August 23, 2021, at https://www.getbengal.com

/details/death-is-not-extinguishing-the-light-it-is-putting-out-the-lamp-as
-dawn-has-come-rabindranath-tagore.

66. Isaiah 49:16, Hebrew Interlinear, accessed August 23, 2021, at https://biblehub
.com/interlinear/isaiah/49-16.htm, and "2710. *chaqaq*," Strong's Concor-
dance, accessed August 23, 2021, at https://biblehub.com/hebrew/2710.htm.

A special thanks to the loving support of my marvelous book agents, Shannon Marven and Jan Miller.

I am always grateful to my LightWorkers team, Chanshi Chibwe and Janet Perez. Thank you to Brian Edwards for his wisdom and his loving friendship, shared with Mark and myself over the years. So grateful, too, for Jerusha Clark and the enthusiasm she brought to embracing these stories so prayerfully and joyfully. My thanks to Suzanne Donahue at Simon & Schuster for believing in this book. And many thanks to the talented Simon & Schuster team: Libby McGuire, Paige Lytle, Jim Thiel, Dana Sloan, and Sonja Singleton. My heartfelt appreciation to each of you for the care and attention to each and every detail of this very special book. And finally, I so value my team at Frank PR. Clare Anne Darragh and Lina Plath are my warrior angels who walk beside me, and I am forever grateful for their friendship.